MAKE ANGER YOUR ALLY

Harnessing Our Most Baffling Emotion

NEIL CLARK WARREN

A DOUBLEDAY-GALILEE BOOK
DOUBLEDAY & COMPANY, INC.
GARDEN CITY, NEW YORK

Galilee Books Edition published July 1985
by special arrangement with Doubleday &
Company, Inc.

Library of Congress Cataloging in Publication Data

Warren, Neil Clark.
    Make anger your ally.

    I. Anger. I. Title.
BF575.A5W37   1983   152.4
ISBN 0-385-23071-0
Library of Congress Catalog Card Number: 82-45933

Make Anger Your Ally

CONTENTS

ACKNOWLEDGMENTS

This book is actually a joint effort. Dozens of people have participated in the development of it, some knowingly and some unknowingly.

Several hundred people at the Bel Air Presbyterian Church and the San Marino Community Church in the Los Angeles area listened and responded to my first attempts at seeing anger as it is—an emotion which has the potential for being used in an enormously destructive or an incredibly helpful way. These loyal partners have for years known the secret of motivating my best effort.

Many of my closest friends have been involved in the project. I asked Loy McGinnis, Rick Thyne, Cliff Penner, Lew Smedes, and Howard and Nell Privett to read a part or all of the manuscript. They gave me honest criticism and warm encouragement.

My clients have, I suppose, taught me the most about the possibility of using anger constructively. I have for twenty years been their pupil for several hours each week. They have shared their sometimes frantic and sometimes victorious attempts to reach a joyful level of living by forming a partnership with their anger.

I talk about these clients throughout this book, but I want to make it clear that I have so scrambled their stories that they are not identifiable. But although the case histories I cite are composites—with names and other details totally altered—these are basically the stories I have heard from week to week in the privacy of my office.

I wish to make special mention of that writer who contributed more to my thinking about anger than anyone else—Professor Albert Bandura of Stanford University. I have read and re-read his book *Aggression: A Social Learning Analysis*, and I highly recommend it to any person who wishes to pursue this subject.

My administrative assistant, Dorie Lott, has participated in every aspect of the writing of this book. She has been available to help on a moment's notice and has given herself enthusiastically in relation to every challenge.

No one has given more energy to the development of this project than my friend Mike Somdal. He is far more than a literary agent. He has mastered the fine art of encouraging and motivating without demanding or alienating.

I have special appreciation for President David Hubbard of Fuller Theological Seminary in Pasadena, California, and the entire faculty of the Graduate School of Psychology who made possible a sabbatical leave during which I could read two hundred articles and books on anger and write to my heart's content in Switzerland—that country which of all countries may well be the most able to use anger constructively in the pursuit of peace.

My wife Marylyn and our daughters, Lorrie, Luann, and Lindsay, listened to nearly every word of this book and contributed emotionally to the enjoyment of the writing process. They are the ones who know how central these ideas are to my own life struggle. To them I am grateful beyond words, and to the four of them I dedicate this book.

N.C.W.

Each year, almost two million American women are severely beaten by their husbands. And surprisingly, an appreciable number of husbands are battered by their wives. Approximately one million children are physically abused by their parents. Further, reports are beginning to surface that many elderly persons are abused by their adult children. Family violence, according to police statistics and research studies, may well be the most common crime in America.

—Editorial, *Theology, News and Notes,* June 1982

Coach Wayne Woodrow Hayes, sixty-five, the autocrat of Ohio State football for twenty-eight years, was fired after assaulting an opposing player. Violent outbursts were a hallmark of his coaching career. "Woody's idea of sublimating," an acquaintance once said, "is to hit someone." . . . The people closest to him never seemed to lose patience. . . . Yet he was always frighteningly—even pathologically—at the mercy of private demons. "When we lose a game, nobody's madder at me than me," he said five years ago. "When I look into the mirror in the morning, I want to take a swing at me." Literally. After losing to Iowa in 1963, Hayes slashed his face with a large ring on his left hand. Pacing the sidelines, he sometimes bit into the fleshy heel of his hand until it bled. Even a heart attack in 1974 did not make Hayes ease up.

—*Time,* January 15, 1979

In America during 1980, there was one violent crime every twenty-four seconds. There was one murder every twenty-three minutes, a total of 82,088 forcible rapes, one robbery every fifty-eight seconds, and one aggravated assault every forty-eight seconds. In the case of murder, the victim was well known to the assailant well over 50 percent of the time, and in these cases angry arguments usually preceded the murderous event.

—*Crime in the United States: Uniform Crime Reports,* Federal Bureau of Investigation

INTRODUCTION

INTRODUCTION—PART 1

When people get angry, the results are almost always negative—even frightful. But it isn't anger's fault. On the contrary, I believe anger is a God-given capacity—a neutral force which offers magnificent possibilities. If people are taught to manage their anger creatively, they can eliminate negative outcomes. In fact, I maintain that when people have learned to use anger constructively, they will be free to experience joy in their lives.

Don't get me wrong. I'm not overlooking the ravaging effects of mishandled anger. I've spent thousands of hours over a number of years talking intimately with people about their problems, and I'm convinced that no problem results in as much pain and consternation as anger does. I've watched one marriage after another fail because two persons didn't know how to use their anger constructively. I've seen patients in fits of rage abuse their children, pick fights with passing motorists, invent schemes to kill themselves—even plan the murders of rejecting spouses or overpowering business associates. Anger management is a shockingly underdeveloped skill in our society.

But it doesn't have to be that way. Our approaches to handling anger are learned, not inherited. They can be altered. I tell my clients: "You can use your anger constructively. In fact, you can become the *master* of your own anger! While anger is an inevitable part of your life, how you use it is up to you. If you learn to take full advantage of your anger, it can help you discover the deepest and most satisfying levels of meaning, both in relationship to others and to yourself."

And then I lead them through the carefully detailed process which is presented in this book. Every step is designed to help a person gain a new degree of leverage in using anger to cope effectively with life. Anger can never be eliminated from a person's experience, but it can be tamed. And then with hard work it can become a dynamic resource in the process of living a full and satisfying life.

INTRODUCTION—PART 2

This book contains a number of ideas about anger and aggression which are radically opposed to common belief. Perhaps you will be shocked more than once as you encounter this new perspective on anger.

There are five points which are fundamental to the system presented here. They are:

1. *Anger is not a primary emotion, but it is typically experienced as an almost automatic inner response to hurt, frustration, or fear.*

All of us have the capacity for anger. It is part of us like breathing is . . . completely natural . . . perfectly legitimate. It is that internal happening which prepares us to cope with hurtful, frustrating, and fearful experiences. Used effectively, anger will assist us significantly in dealing with the pain sources in our lives.

2. *Anger is physiological arousal. It is nothing more.*

This statement is significantly different from the common understanding. Most people mix "anger" up with all kinds of other terms. And their "traveling definition" of anger is often corrupted beyond recognition.

Anger is simply a physical state of readiness. When we are angry, we are prepared to act. This is all anger is—preparedness.

The value of anger is determined by how it is expressed. It can be used to make things right or to destroy everything and everyone in sight. How anger is used is independent of what anger is.

3. *Anger and aggression are significantly different.*

More often than not, people draw no distinction between anger and aggression. They think of someone who is angry as a person who is waving his or her hands, talking loudly, spitting out all sorts of bitter words, maybe even on the verge of being physical.

That describes some aspects of one type of anger *expression* referred to as aggression. When a description of aggression is confused with the definition of "anger," it's no wonder so many people think of anger in a negative way.

Let me say it again: Anger is simply physiological preparedness. It gives you the capacity to act in relation to whatever is wrong, whatever has you upset.

Aggression is almost always destructive. It is a tragedy for anger to be used in the service of aggression. It's like throwing your finest resource away . . . like using nuclear energy to destroy people when it could be used to make life more abundant for millions.

I am opposed to almost all aggressive behavior. I take the position throughout this book that aggression usually has long-term negative consequences. I stand against *all* anger expression which is solely designed to inflict physical or psychological pain on another. I argue against every variety of bitterness, meanness, and ridicule—whether it is delivered verbally or physically.

4. *How we use our anger is learned.*

This opens up an unlimited set of possibilities. It means this: However you have expressed your anger in the past can be altered. You can learn completely new ways of putting your anger to work for you. You can literally make anger your most productive ally.

What we know from careful psychological research is that most people learn to express their anger when they are very young. The learning process is largely characterized by two phenomena: modeling and reinforcement.

Modeling involves your observing other persons express their anger. Perhaps you studied a parent, older sibling, friend, or television personality.

Most violent persons have been subjected to one or more violent models. A high percentage of these persons come from homes in which a member of the family was violent. But newspapers and entertainment programs are filled with aggressively expressed anger also. Studies have demonstrated that violence on television occurs at the rate of approximately seven assaults an hour, and over 80 percent of all programming contains some violence.

Reinforcement simply refers to the immediate consequences of behavior. In our culture anger expressed aggressively is regularly reinforced. People change when they get yelled at— at least for a few minutes—but yelling usually produces long-term negative results. The learned behavior pattern, however, acquired when we are young, is little affected by the long-term outcome.

5. *The expression of anger can come under your control.*

Through the disciplined use of your rational powers, you can develop the ability to use your anger to cope effectively with major problems in your life.

This book will assist you in mobilizing your capacity to think under stress. You will learn how to dissolve habituated and destructive ways of expressing your anger. And then you can learn to substitute new behavioral sequences designed to resolve problems and create possibilities for meaningful experiences of productive and satisfying living.

Those are my main points.

And they all lead to this: Anger offers a wide variety of possibilities. It can create chaos in your life, or you can learn to express it in highly constructive ways. It can provide all the power you need to remove troublesome barriers in your path. You can move forward methodically when you have learned to use anger effectively.

But becoming an expert in the management of anger requires hard work . . . concentrated work. You can get all the ideas you need from this book. And if you follow them up with regular practice, you will learn to harness this emotion for those constructive purposes which are fundamental in your life.

ANGER—KING OF LIFE'S CHALLENGES

Since everybody has a body that automatically prepares for action in the face of life's provoking events, everybody has anger. Anger is the coiling of the spring in you, an intricately designed internal process which gives you the capacity to manage the difficult and threatening parts of your life.

It happens in all of us. We get angry. Thank goodness! If we didn't, we would be defenseless in the face of every kind of hurt and frustration. When we're angry, we have enormous power available. And what we choose to do with that power can move us like a missile to a place of resolution and peace or to the point of destruction.

Most people simply don't know what to do with all that power. They have received virtually no help with it from parents, teachers, friends, minister, or family doctor. They are almost always baffled and confused by it. They're tired of being angry so often—and ending up feeling so helpless in handling it wisely.

They need to use their anger effectively so they can get on with caring for each other. And that's what this book is about —anger transformed, anger turned into an ally. Section I is about the mismanagement of anger—the ways it typically gets us into trouble. In Section II I clarify the issues connected with anger. I make sure you understand exactly what anger is, where it comes from, and what it was designed to accomplish. As you read these first two sections, you will have questions about your own anger and how to handle it. You may wonder if I'm *ever* going to start answering *your* questions instead of raising even more on my own.

You can be sure that the answers to your questions will become available. For Section III contains the most detailed plan ever published about how to master your anger.

You know what a dangerous emotion we're trying to master. It's common knowledge that:

—If you pretend you have no anger and try to bury it, it can bury you—literally—by triggering a heart attack or a stroke.

—If you let it out in the wrong way, it can ruin your marriage, alienate your children, or get you fired.

—If you somehow get it turned around on yourself, it can tear your self-image apart, destroy your self-esteem, and set you up for all kinds of psychic pain.

—If you fail to process it when you experience it, it may turn to resentment; and if it does, you can become hostile, negative, and impossible to be around.

Anger is incredibly tough to control and use wisely. I know that from painful personal experience. It's an emotion I've had a hard time transforming in my own life.

The word anger was loaded with negative connotations in the environment in which I grew up. It was inappropriate to be angry. If I did get angry, guilt was only a half step behind.

There was virtually no appreciation of the possibility that anger could be used constructively. Actually, as far as I can recall, I never once had anyone spend two minutes tutoring me about the positive uses of anger.

I was taught to deny my anger, pretend I had none, cover it over so completely that I could fool everyone, including me.

So that's what I did—as well as I knew how—and I had a considerable amount of success.

But when I eventually discovered that the capacity for anger is a natural part of my biological makeup, I was relieved. The idea that anger expression is learned, that it can be modified with practice, was totally new and untested for me long after I became an adult.

Now I know the consequences that disciplined effort in this area can have. I've discovered firsthand the rewards of constructively expressed anger. When we are angry, all the power of our person is available to us. We become equipped to act decisively in the interests of resolution and healing. Instead of creating trouble for ourselves, we can use anger to cope with the pain sources we encounter. Rather than trying to deny our anger, we can learn to manage it with the skill of a professional.

That's the formidable challenge this book addresses—and the promise is a payoff well worth the tremendous effort which anger mastery will require of us.

Make Anger Your Ally

SECTION I

Common Strategies for Mismanaging Anger

Me? A Problem with Anger?

Fundamental to the development of effective anger management is a detailed recognition of how you handle your anger. The essential question is whether anger is a problem for you.

If you fly off the handle periodically, or fear you might, or live with someone who does, anger is a continual threat. It comes out of the blue—desk pounding, face slapping, loud cussing, bitter put-downs. I call these people "exploders."

It doesn't matter which side of those explosions you're on. You've got a problem.

If you *never* get angry and never have, you may still have a significant problem with anger.

Especially if you have ulcers, high blood pressure, headaches, or pain of "undetermined cause." You are a "somatizer." You are using your body—your soma—as a way to express your anger. And if you are, look out.

Or you may be one of those low-key people who never gets angry, but you're chronically depressed. You climb all over yourself for the smallest mistakes, and every time you do, you suffocate your spirit. You are a "self-punisher." It doesn't matter that you don't mean to, or that you don't know you're doing it. The fact is that you're depressed a lot—and your way of handling anger is probably to blame.

If you live with a depressed person, you know how frustrating that can be. One minute you're worried sick about them, and the next minute you'd like to take them behind the shed. Their anger—expressed so inadequately—makes you burn.

Plenty of other "I never get angry" people use anger in ways which require magicians to detect, but you can't miss the feeling of daggers in the air. I refer to these people as "underhanders."

In their slick, almost invisible way, they pursue their target relentlessly. They can strike in a hundred different ways. Some of them try to depress other people. They throw out barely camouflaged negative barbs about your weekend plans or your child's teacher or your minister or your husband's boss or your husband. Their anger invariably sneaks out. They've got an anger problem whether they know it or not.

Of course, there are countless other underhanders—pouters and bad losers and your-faulters and poor-me'ers. If you're one of these or you live with one, anger is a problem for you.

And your community is full of angry people who have to be handled by you—the speeding drivers who risk their lives and yours every corner they cut; the purse snatchers and house burglars and rapists who would rather *use* you than deal constructively with their own anger; the charlatan business people who would cheat you if you didn't watch every move.

The shadow of anger is on every moment for some of us. If you hit your kids or your wife, or get hit by your dad or your mom or your husband, anger problems haunt you day and night.

The fact is that most of us handle our anger artlessly, often making tense situations even more difficult. Instead of anger assisting us in moving toward our goals, it becomes one of our major problems. Sometimes we are foggy about the role of anger in our lives. It's difficult for us to get a clear picture of what we're like when we're angry. The purpose of Section I is to give you a look at some people I have known who tried to handle anger in one of these four ways. I suggest you compare their strategies with your own. See if you find yourself in any of these categories.

STRATEGY NUMBER 1—
EXPLODING

Sometimes I Just Lose My Cool

"Sure I get angry sometimes." Jerry Lynch tried to make me understand. "When I come home, I just want some peace and quiet. The kids get to yelling and screaming and running all over the place. I usually warn them once or twice. And if they keep it up, sometimes I just lose my cool."

Jerry was a thirty-two-year-old carpenter—a short, stout man, deeply tanned, with a tattoo on his left forearm.

"I work so hard on the job every day. And with all that work, there's never enough money. The kids always need something or the car goes bad or the roof springs a leak. I'm under a lot of pressure."

Jerry had been "encouraged" to see me by his wife, Kathy. His flare-ups had been occurring more often during the last few months, and she was frightened. On two occasions, during blowups, Jerry had been totally out of control. She had finally gotten up the courage to call an old friend of hers, a minister in a nearby town. He had referred her to me for help.

Kathy told me a lot about Jerry in two sessions. "All our friends love him," she said. "He's one of the nicest guys in the world most of the time, and then all of a sudden, out of the blue, he explodes. When he does, he shouts and swears, and lately, he's been hitting the kids with his fists a lot. He's made some frightening threats to me too. He's lost two jobs because of his temper, and I think he's in trouble on this one too."

When Jerry came to me, he told me his history. His dad was a long-distance trucker—a tough "loner" who was gone most of the time when Jerry was growing up. Jerry idolized his dad, but his dad paid little attention to him. At times, his dad would discipline him with a belt and the experience frightened Jerry.

His mother was a strong Christian woman who took him and his younger brother and sister to church at least twice and sometimes three times a week.

When he was young, he got into fights a lot, Jerry told me. "It happened once in a Sunday school class at church, and I remember the teacher keeping me for at least a half hour after class talking to me. He told me that God doesn't want us to get angry—that it's a sin—and that I should work to get rid of my temper. From that time on for a long time I got in only one or two fights. But I still got mad a lot. It took all I had to keep from fighting."

Jerry and Kathy married when he was nineteen and she was eighteen. Things went pretty well at first.

"Shortly after Chuckie was born though" —Jerry spoke slowly now, as if he was remembering this for the first time in years— "she began to complain that I never seemed to care about her. She said I cut her down all the time, that I was sarcastic a lot. Over the months, she got so worked up about it that we saw a marriage counselor.

"We only saw him four or five times. He said he thought I had a lot of anger down in me. He kept telling me to 'get with it and get it out.' He explained to me that if I didn't 'let it fly' when I felt it, I'd get it out later in a more destructive way.

"So that's what I've been trying to do—get it out when I feel it. And now Kathy is all upset again . . . threatening to leave me if I don't get my temper under control.

"The church told me not to let myself be mad, and the counselor told me to let it fly. Who am I supposed to believe?"

Letting Anger Out Explosively

Jerry Lynch was in deep trouble because he regularly exploded when he was angry. He had lost two jobs, put two of his kids in the emergency room, and seriously risked his marriage because he "couldn't control himself."

At least in those wild, fitful moments it seemed as if he couldn't control himself—as if there was no harnessing that frightful power in him.

The pattern is fairly typical. First, there's the setting event. You're worn out or discouraged or unhappy. Things haven't been going right for you "this afternoon" or "this week" or "since we moved here" or "for as long as I can remember."

And then there's the triggering event. Sometimes you can feel it coming—maybe even "see" it coming. Your kids won't behave. Your boss won't let up. Your wife won't quit nagging. The traffic won't move. The car won't start again. The bill collector called for the third time today. It could be any one of a million things.

The adrenaline begins to flow. You feel your teeth clench. Your muscles flex. Your stomach tightens. Your heart beats faster. Your hands become more like fists. Your neck and forehead get hot. You are coiled.

For a split second you try not to erupt. You have a distant inkling you should walk away, cool down, keep control. But she just keeps nagging. And pow! You go off! The trigger has been pulled. The hammer is heading for the firing pin.

Sometimes the explosion comes in slow motion. Your consciousness picks up bits and pieces of the wildness. "I know I'm in the middle of this thing. I'm just going to get this taken care of right now. I think I know what I'm doing."

And once in a while there's the little voice in your head that says: "That's enough." "You've hurt her." "You're hitting him too hard." "Look out. Things are getting away from you."

But sometimes you can't stop, or you don't want to, or you're afraid to. You just keep talking or hitting or chasing or threatening. Your mouth or your arms or your feet are in automatic now. It's not you anymore. It's your machine out of control. A wild set of habits you learned when you were four has taken command.

Then you experience a tiny sense of cooling off. You don't feel quite as wild or tense. You start to "see" more of what is going on. You're still too hot to think, but not hot enough to keep yelling or swinging.

You slow down noticeably now. There's a surge of consciousness. You relax your hands a little. You close your mouth. You try to swallow. There's a silence about you.

Your breathing is still jerky. You can still feel the blood coursing through your arms and legs. Your eyes are wide. But you step back a bit.

And during the next few minutes or hours, you replay the scene dozens of times. At first, you try to justify your actions, but you know it's useless, and you quit making alibis.

You try to think about what triggered your outburst. You encounter some amnesia. What you know is that you went out of control. It didn't matter in that second where you were, what you were doing, or who you were with. You wanted to let 'em have it—make them feel bad like you were feeling.

But if you're like most exploders, you begin to forget after a while. No real change takes place in you. You've got a pattern going.

And anger explosions come in many forms.

Letting It Fly Verbally

Anger explosions proceed most often from the mouth. And that spray of verbal lead can be as deadly as a machine gun.

These explosions usually have several objectives, but their ultimate purpose is nearly always the same: to punish the target, hit him between the eyes, do him in. Whether the words are designed to place blame, to justify an action, or to let another person know that you won't take anymore, they usually involve a high percentage of poisonous put-down. "I want to make that guy feel bad, make him wrong, make him pay."

What are these verbal explosions all about? They're almost always about unmet needs—needs to feel complete or perfect or secure.

And verbal bombshells are usually directed at those people most important to the meeting of your needs. If you find yourself exploding regularly at a person, ask yourself what needs you think that person is failing to meet for you. A careful assessment of those needs is often embarrassingly revealing. Much of the time they are "fantasy needs" from our most irrational centers.

Sometimes we unconsciously assume that our needs, as we perceive them, should *always* get met. The whole world should revolve around us, nurture us, and keep us satisfied. When that doesn't happen, we feel wronged. We blame the other person—so we let loose with a carefully chosen set of "put-downers." What we want to say, even though we could never reveal this much irrationality, is: "Pay very close attention to meeting my needs *all* the time. That's what should matter most to you."

And sometimes we have an unconscious need to be seen as perfect. Social approval becomes like a god for us. And we seem to operate on the assumption that that approval requires perfection. Since criticism indicates flaw, and flaw jeopardizes approval, we explode in response to the slightest critical remark about us. So great is its threat to that fragile psychic structure of ours which is erected on our ability to secure other people's approval of us by our being good enough.

Some professionals have argued that verbal anger-sprays are healthy and should be encouraged. "It gets it off your chest," they say, "and uses up your slush fund." By this they mean that if you verbally let your anger fly, you will get rid of excess "aggressive energy" and be less likely to show aggression in the future.

But that isn't what careful psychological research suggests. First, there's almost certainly no such thing as a "slush fund" of "aggressive energy." Research findings cast considerable doubt on the energy idea in general, and certainly on the concept of energy accumulation.

More importantly, the overwhelming majority of psychological research on anger expression makes it clear that aggressive behavior facilitates more aggressive behavior rather than less.

So to explode with words almost always stimulates further words from your "opponent"—or fists. In a 1980 study of American domestic violence, *Behind Closed Doors,* by Straus, Gelles, and Steinmetz,[1] over 80 percent of those couples who

---

[1] M. A. Straus, R. J. Gelles, and S. K. Steinmetz, *Behind Closed Doors* (Garden City, N.Y.: Anchor Press/Doubleday, 1981).

used verbal abuse with one another ended up in physical combat.

I have seldom experienced verbal outbursts as having any constructive long-term value except in the most guarded professional setting. These eruptions almost always lead to new hurt and added threat.

But sometimes, in the heat of the moment when our body is burning, it feels so reasonable to let fly with a verbal left and right to the ear. Whether it's our spouse or our kids, our opponent or our colleague, our boss or our subordinate, or even our god—if they haven't been performing up to expectation in meeting our needs, or if they've been demanding more of us and finding us inadequate, we just want to hit them squarely. Something in us presses hard to let our anger out, even though the gain will be very short-term, and the loss may hound us for a long time.

For instance, take Sharon Kelly who blew up at her boss. She had been upset with him for several weeks, and she finally just told him what she thought of him. He was shocked, and his decision came immediately. Two weeks later, Sharon was job hunting.

She enjoyed the experience of telling him off. She liked the feeling of "getting it all out" and of "being cleansed" of all that resentment she had built up. At least she liked it till the middle of the night after she let loose. When she awoke at two-fifteen in the morning, she thought of nothing else until it was time to get up. And as she reflected, she began to think of other ways she could have handled her feelings.

She also started thinking about the loss she was going to experience in giving up that job—all the people she felt close to there, the excellent pay, the chance for advancement, the good working conditions. She didn't want to leave.

But in reality, Sharon had made the decision when she blew up. She no longer had a choice. She had opted for a short-term gain, and now she was experiencing a long-term loss. In my experience, that's the tragic error which people most commonly make.

Explosions from the mouth, whether they are part of a hit-and-run action or a long, brutal beating with words, ought to be labeled for what they are: "Aggression—Dangerous to Any Important Relationship You May Have."

The Consequences of
Letting Anger Out Explosively

Angry outbursts lead to a wide variety of consequences.
Very few are positive. Most are negative.

For instance, on the positive side I have known of break-
throughs to occur between people on the heels of a serious
blowup between them. It has almost always seemed to me
that the blowup was not in itself very helpful, but the expressions of feeling in the interests of recovering from the blowup
seemed the central healing factor.

Moreover, I have known people who, on the basis of a
blowup, were able to break off destructive relationships which
they should have left years earlier. And I have seen some people right some longtime wrongs in a moment of inner heat
and passion.

But during my years as a psychotherapist, I have witnessed
far more negative consequences from anger outbursts. In fact,
I have rank-ordered ten of these negative consequences from
the most likely occurrence to the least likely. You may also
find them to be in the reverse order of their seriousness. But
that will depend on what particular values you espouse.

1. *Personal embarrassment and the need for a pride-*

crunching apology. This is the most likely and least serious consequence.

"I am really sorry about last night. I have no idea what came over me. On reflection, I was stunned by my own behavior."

Or "I am mortified when I think about what I did to you yesterday. That came from a place in me that I abhor. What I said about you is not at all the way I feel toward you."

These are expensive moments and, obviously, their success will depend on their infrequency.

2. *The more damaged relationship* is next. Perhaps you know all about long periods of awkward and unsatisfying relating with that person who was the object of your harsh words or behavior.

If it's your spouse, it can last for a day or much longer. It depends on what you did and where. These are painful periods. Sexual expression may vanish. Conversation may slacken. It's cold and quiet punishment, and both of you end up feeling wounded.

3. *The termination of friendship*. It isn't always obvious at first. Things can seem to be patched up. But you begin to sense a change. She has a party without telling you about it. She's never done that before. He's playing in a new tennis group, and he didn't mention it. Strange. And the friendship begins a long, slow process of deterioration.

Of course, that process can also be abrupt. You just never have contact with each other again.

But abrupt or gradual, the friendship got damaged beyond repair by the aggressive words or the uncontrolled behavior.

4. *A significant job consequence*. I suppose millions of secretaries have quit, partners have "divorced," and workmen have lost their jobs because of anger eruptions. Sometimes these terminations are part of a much larger picture. But sometimes the way a person handles

his or her anger leads all by itself to serious employment disruptions.

5. *Costly damage to property.* The following story caught
   my attention:

   International Herald Tribune, January 19, 1982. A man in
   Bellevue, Washington, was driven to "autocide" by Washington's first major winter storm. That's what Bellevue Police
   Major Jack Kellem called the strange case of an irate motorist who beat, then shot his car after it got stuck in six inches
   of snow. Police said the man became so angry when his ve-
   hicle got stuck that he pulled a tire iron from the trunk and
   smashed all the windows. Then he hauled out a pistol and
   shot all four tires, reloaded, and emptied half of a second
   clip of bullets into the car. "He killed it," Kellem said. "It's
   a case of autocide." Kellem said the man was sober and rational but very perturbed.

6. *Runaways.* I can still remember one of my early therapy
   cases as if it were yesterday. A father got wildly aggressive with his son one night—read him out and threatened all kinds of punishment. The next morning there
   was a note on the boy's bed. He had decided to leave.
       Sure it was his way of striking back. But he stayed
   away—has never yet returned, as far as I know. The father has regretted his action a thousand times, but the
   result remains the same.

7. *Guilt* sponges up all the self-esteem some people can
   produce. If you feel that your anger explosion has resulted in physical pain or injury for another person, or a
   broken relationship with someone who really mattered
   to you, you may experience pervasive and unyielding
   inner guilt.

8. *Divorce.* I've seen several marriages sunk by massive
   displays of uncontrolled anger. You might be saying,
   "Those marriages must have been pretty far gone anyway." Sometimes that was true, but not always. Too
   many times I've watched marriages that still had a good

chance terminated because one or both parties "let it all fly."

9. *Anxiety* is often the result of threats which are made during an episode of anger. When one person "promises to get" another, or when the loser says things such as "You'll pay for this" or "You haven't heard the end of this by a long way," it can strike terror in the heart of the hearers, especially if the threat is made by a powerful person or one very likely to follow through.

10. You might guess that number ten would be *murder or personal injury*. I have had clients beaten up (both children and adults) when another family member went into a fit of rage. I have watched those injuries change the victims' personalities and wound them emotionally for life.

     I have had to stop clients from beating up one another when their anger erupted in blows designed to punish. And my associates have had clients murdered by spouses or other acquaintances—almost always as a result of anger explosions.

Once in a great while, the consequences of explosive anger, as I said, can sometimes be positive. Certain psychologists have made this form of anger expression a central part of their therapeutic approach.

But the overwhelming majority of what I've witnessed has been devastatingly negative. In Section III I'll describe some highly productive ways to take advantage of the tremendous power anger provides.

Therapy for an Exploder—
A Preview of Anger Management

Gary Sheridan was a baseball player. He called me for an appointment one October, soon after the league season was over. "I need to work on my temper," Gary told me, "and I heard you're interested in working with people who have problems like mine."

His anger was destroying his career and causing him all kinds of trouble at home. He had gotten into three fights or near fights on the field. He regularly yelled at his wife and children. On two occasions he walked out of the general manager's office. And one situation, the last one, especially frightened him. He hit an opposing player in the chin during a fight and broke his jaw. The player threatened to sue, and the papers wrote a long story about Gary's temper.

We narrowed the specific provocative events to six: (1) When a pitcher would throw too close to his head after another player on his team had hit a home run; (2) When an opponent slid into second base to break up a double play and seemed to be trying to injure Gary, who was a shortstop; (3) When he would strike out in the late innings with runners on base and his team tied or slightly behind; (4) When his children made a lot of noise the morning after a night game; (5)

When his wife complained about the insecurity surrounding their living conditions because of his job; (6) When the general manager made disparaging remarks about some aspect of his play in an effort to justify his offer of a lower salary than Gary was asking for.

I saw Gary only ten times, but he worked unusually hard on his problem during that period.

Early on, he recognized how he became an exploder. When he was eight or nine, he started playing Little League baseball. He was always talented, but his dad, who was one of the coaches, thought some of the larger kids regularly took advantage of him. He encouraged Gary to be aggressive. "You may have to pop 'em one when they do that to you," he would tell him after a pitcher had thrown close to him. When Gary didn't act aggressively, his dad derided him and intimated he was a coward.

Gary remembered the first time he tried anything aggressive. He slid into third after a long hit. It was a close play, and the third baseman tagged him out. As Gary was walking away, the other player laughed at him. Gary flared, came back, and started a fight. His dad told him that night he was proud of him. And Gary felt tougher than he had before.

But now that style of anger expression had become a serious handicap. He wanted to extinguish it and replace it with some new habits.

I knew our job was easier than it might have been if he had developed the habit at an earlier age and had less cognitive understanding of it. But no behavior which had been reinforced as often as his had was going to be that easy to alter.

We began to work in five basic areas:

1. I asked him to spell out in writing the kind of man he wanted to be, in terms of anger expression. And before he completed that task, I encouraged him to read three books on anger I had available.

    I didn't accept his first effort. It was his third draft we finally agreed to keep.

Then I asked him to commit himself to read that statement aloud every Monday to his wife. He agreed to do that.

2. I coached him on staying in close touch with his feelings —especially in the "vicinity" of these provocative events.

The goal was for him to catch his explosive buildup at the first sign—before it got away from him. We went over dozens of anger episodes he had experienced. We broke them down into detailed parts. We began to pick up the pattern. He came to know some things to look for.

3. We worked on *delaying* responses once the early feelings had been detected. I stressed that it took great discipline to choose an alternate route at the critical juncture in the anger process, because he had been conditioned to expect a positive result from the aggressive behavior. Since his life had been built around discipline, he responded quickly to the challenge. The key word at the earliest sign was "think." Every time we rehearsed one of the anger episodes, when we reached the critical zone, we obsessed over "think."

4. He was to think about two questions: What do I want from this encounter? And how can I get what I want most effectively?

We worked out answers to all six provocative situations. For instance, in connection with the beanball experience, he concluded that what he wanted most was to keep his cool, hit the ball hard, and perhaps start a rally. And he concluded that his strategy would be to use all the potential of his aroused state to concentrate on the pitcher and the pitch, and then to swing naturally if and when he got his pitch.

5. I worked with Gary on his own expectations. Sometimes he expected too much from himself and from his family. We clarified the reasonableness of three kids making some noise at nine-thirty in the morning, of his wife needing considerable support in relation to the ever-present threat of their moving, of the general manager

wanting to hold his costs down, and we spent one whole hour on Gary's expectations for himself in relation to baseball.

We did several other things too (all of which will be elaborated in Section III), including the setting up of an anger journal. Gary committed himself to recording all the experiences of anger he had over the next six months, on the days he had them. The reminding event was getting into bed every night. Before climbing in, he would take out his journal and record several pertinent facts about any experience with anger which he had had that day.

The fascinating thing for me was to see the progress a person with great discipline could make in changing a behavior pattern which had become a significant problem for him.

After two baseball seasons, he reported that he had been involved in no fights or near fights, he had recently signed a five-year contract after an anger-free set of negotiations, he had mastered the substitute response at the first sign of anger, and his relationships at home were significantly better. Moreover, his batting average had improved.

I am convinced that anger can be used constructively in the interests of valued objectives.

It is critical to remember that aggression is only one form of anger expression—and virtually always a highly disappointing one.

With sufficient inner discipline and a solid training program, aggressive behavior can be eliminated, and substitute behaviors can be learned.

I Get What I Ask for but Not What I Want

Anger explosions almost always get results. In fact, that's how we learned these "hard to give up" patterns in the first place. Nearly every time we let fly with our anger something changes, and we experience a sense of relief for a moment or two. So we get reinforced for our outbursts.

What changes as a result of our tantrums? People do. Most people are properly frightened by a lot of raw anger. They try to do whatever they can to make it stop.

If they were nagging before you started yelling, you can be sure they will stop nagging. If they weren't paying attention before you shook them, they will carefully watch you now. If they were playing the radio too loudly before you began pounding on their door, they will leap up to turn it down. If you're mad because they haven't been caring enough about you, they will start "caring" about you more.

But most likely, whether you know it or not at the time, you're not really looking for behavioral obedience. You're looking for more genuine appreciation of your thoughts and feelings, more sensitivity to your needs, more love for your person.

And that's almost certainly what you're not going to get

from yelling and pounding. Your "target" is more likely to be filled with resentment and disrespect in response to that kind of treatment. To be sure, it will be secret resentment and disrespect. There's no way they want to trigger that wildness in you again.

And so the relief you feel in that first moment or two will be hollow and short-lived. Actually, things will probably get worse rather than better. Explosions inevitably increase the potential for counterattack. But you won't know that for a while.

When you come to know it, you will realize that you got what you asked for but hardly what you wanted.

I've had many a client who had to learn this painful lesson over and over again. When the outburst pattern gets set in place, it is repeatedly validated by the minimal reinforcement from that first minute of anxious compliance. This validation makes it ever harder for the exploder to break free of verbal or physical attack strategies.

Ted Mitchell was a stockbroker who came to me because his life was falling apart. He was under heavy pressure at home and at the office. He explained to me that his highly consistent response to that pressure revolved around his short fuse and his high energy level. When he let fly, he was apparently frightening.

As he told me about that pattern, he seemed eager to convince me of how well it was working for him. He brought traders into line that way. He regularly "motivated" his secretary by firing off at her, controlled his kids, got the most from his wife, and he even thought he did better at golf when he threw his clubs.

But Ted was a smart man. It didn't take long for him to see that his kids tried not to be around him, his wife was threatening to leave him, he had had three secretaries in eighteen months, traders often didn't return his calls, and his golf score was actually no better now than when he first joined the country club nearly five years earlier.

It was true that his kids were quieter around him, his secretary harder-working, the traders more definitive about prices (when they called back), his wife more productive, and his golf game more serious.

But the penalties corresponding to each of those gains made the gains seem cheap and unimportant.

Anger displays often work. You get what you ask for—at least for a few minutes. But you usually make what you really want significantly harder to achieve.

The positive, long-term results which Gary Sheridan—the baseball player—experienced came only from disciplined effort and a carefully developed plan. The secret is to take full control of the way anger is expressed—and to use that control to eliminate explosions and substitute far more effective behaviors. This type of plan is spelled out in careful detail in Section III of this book.

STRATEGY NUMBER 2—
SOMATIZING

In the last several chapters I have talked about exploders. They are the most obvious of the anger mismanagers, but there are other easily identifiable types. I want to talk about somatizers, those people whose bodies show the riddled effects of knifelike anger.

My Body's a Mess,
but I'm Not Angry

Joan Williams' first words caught me off guard. "No offense, but I don't expect much to come of this. You're the last in a series of psychologists and psychiatrists I've seen since I was fifteen. The others haven't helped me much, and frankly, I don't expect it to be any better this time." She seemed to enjoy telling me that.

"I'm not sure then why you're here," I said.

"Dr. James thought you might be able to help me. He's my internist. I've seen him for years. He's always suspected my physical problems were related to my emotional life, and he says he's even more concerned about that now."

Joan went on to tell me about a series of physical ailments she had suffered with, any one of which could have made life miserable. She had headaches when she was in high school which were so bad she missed a lot of school. She always suffered excessively from menstrual cramps. And now, shortly after her thirtieth birthday, Dr. James had diagnosed her stomach problems as a severe case of ulcers.

She also told me in some detail about her failing marriage. "He put me down," she said of her husband, "and he has kept me there for years." She also chronicled some of the happenings at work, where she perceived that her employer took continual advantage of her.

Joan was a tall, beautiful woman. But although attractive, there was something hard about her. Her mind worked like a computer. She fed the data in, and it was processed from a highly rational perspective, then returned. In fact, almost never did I say anything to her which seemed to strike her as something she hadn't already encountered and worked through.

Joan professed to want help but seemed convinced there wasn't any to be had. And I suspected she would resist discovering her assessment wrong.

As she talked about her family, her deep sense of resentment became more and more obvious. Both her mother and husband had tried to shape her, to impose their will on her. She thought they often conspired with one another. Together, she concluded, they had managed to ruin her life.

But she denied any anger toward them. They had done their best, she supposed. "But more importantly," she said, "I don't get angry, and I don't hold grudges—ever. Sometimes I get upset with people, but not angry."

She was honest about that; she consciously experienced no anger. But after working with scores of people, I had come to trust my feelings. She came on like barbed wire with dozens of sharp "picks" designed to rip and tear. I felt continually on trial with her, ill at ease, unaccepted. She reported that she had few friends—they didn't seem to have much to give her that she wanted. I began to suspect that with her superior intelligence, she was able to cover her razorlike edges so well that people didn't know why they didn't want to be around her. They just didn't.

But that same barbed wire was rubbing against her too and making her body a mass of raw wounds.

Her mother, a highly energized, dominating lady, had taught her early in life that you should never be angry. And she had taught her so well that even strong feelings of resentment were completely denied. The pattern had persisted for so long that these feeling centers were anesthetized by now. Her feelings and her consciousness had become detached, and she suffered without understanding why.

Joan was a victim of anger that, left unprocessed, used her body as a way of expressing itself. In fact, when she was growing up, she had discovered that having something wrong with your body was perfectly legitimate. She had actually been reinforced with additional attention and concern from her mother during these periods. And so, along with thousands of others, she adopted that unconscious "strategy" which resulted in horrendous physical suffering. Massive resentment was the underlying emotion in her psychosomatic symptom development. Her body had become the target and the voice of her rage.

Resentment Is Like Acid
in Our Bodies

When we allow resentment to fester in us, we are setting ourselves up for serious trouble. It has an effect on the tissues of our body similar to that of acid. It produces physical pathology.

Luborsky, Docherty, and Penick[1] published a revealing article in *Psychosomatic Medicine* in 1973. They carefully reviewed a sample of fifty-seven studies in an effort to detect which psychological conditions existed for people prior to the onset of psychosomatic symptoms.

Resentment was that inner condition most frequently discovered to be connected with these punishing ailments. And frustration, closely related to resentment, was in second place.

How does resentment create such destruction? Feelings of resentment undoubtedly do not exist in some energy form within our bodies as some have theorized. Rather, resentment apparently wears away at our bodies as a function of what we think.

For instance, if we take what someone says to us as an in-

[1] L. Luborsky, J. P. Docherty, and S. Penick, "Onset conditions for psychosomatic symptoms: A comparative review of immediate observation with retrospective research." *Psychosomatic Medicine*, 1973, 35, 187–204.

sult, we will experience some hurt—and that hurt may be transformed into resentment toward that person who delivered what we perceived to be an insult. Physically, our anger prepares us for action. We then have the capacity to process the insult—to work with it and relate to the source of it until we have neutralized it.

But what happens if we fail to use our anger to work through our feelings about the insult? What happens if we walk away from the situation just as hurt as we were at the beginning? What happens is that every time we think about what that person said to us, we feel hurt and resentful all over again. And our body prepares each time to do something, to provide the power to move effectively against the source of the pain. But we repeatedly fail to use the resources which are available. And the hurt feelings remain.

If we ruminate over negative experiences like this one, which may have occurred months or even years earlier, experiences we have never managed to neutralize by working them through, our bodies become aroused time after time. This repetitive process is extremely wearing and cannot be endured by most people without the development of physiological pathology.

Resentment, then, is the source of an enormous amount of suffering. Our bodies buckle under the strain of a persistent state of preparedness necessitated by an unresolved hurt.

But resentment can be dissolved. Actually, anger—the word we use to denote the physiological preparedness we spoke about above—can be used to deal effectively with that original insulting event. I'll show you how to do that later in this book. There is simply no need to let resentment cause so much physical pain and suffering.

It Can Chew on Your Insides

Our bodies are amazing creations. And we know significantly more about how they operate than we did fifty years ago.

We know that the interactions between our emotions and our physiological processes are highly complex and extremely influential in both directions. How a person relates to others and to life in general can both determine certain physical events and be an effect of one or more of them.

And we have learned that our bodily functioning is regulated by two nervous systems—the sympathetic and the parasympathetic. The sympathetic nervous system is the emergency system which prepares us to deal with many kinds of immediate concerns. When this system is activated, our heart beats faster, our blood pressure is increased, adrenaline is secreted more rapidly, more sugar is released into our system, our muscles tense, and our external arteries constrict. All our reserves are available, and we are ready for almost anything. It is this sympathetic nervous system which is responsive to events (internal and external) we have come to label as troubling or threatening—in need of immediate attention. And when the sympathetic system is aroused, we are what we call "angry."

The important point is this: When we are angry and we fail to resolve the situation which has triggered our anger—what I call our pain source—two problems may create future difficulties for us:

1. The specific situation which we have not resolved may continue to confront us. If we can't extricate ourselves from it, the sympathetic arousal system may continue on a state of alert.

2. Even if we can remove ourselves physically from the situation by miles or years, our memory may continue to replay the problematic experience for us. And as we mentioned in the last chapter, our bodies may get reactivated every time that happens.

When this happens frequently enough, there is physiological deterioration. Twenty or more physical conditions are thought to be affected by unprocessed anger. Let me mention five of the common ones:

1. *Headaches.* There are many causes of headaches. Frequent headaches deserve both medical and psychological evaluation.

   One of the most common causes is tension. When your body is activated by anger, you are prepared for war with primitive forces. Your whole musculature is rigid and ready.

   If it is maintained in this condition, many disorders can result. Headaches are experienced by millions of Americans who have not been able to resolve the situations which cause them pain—nor have they been able to turn off their physiological emergency system.

2. *Stomach problems.* I have had many persons referred to me by their internists because of stomach ulcers apparently related to emotional disorders. In fact, in America today ulcers and emotional concerns are auto-

matically linked in most people's thinking. The pain of an ulcerated stomach is sometimes the first signal some persons have detected in themselves that they have psychological problems. A person who comes for help with his stomach may leave with a new anger-expression strategy which will benefit his life in significant other areas.

3. *Colds.* The common cold probably accounts for as much total pain every year as any other single ailment. And some colds are undoubtedly related to inadequately expressed anger.

How might that be? If it is true that we always have cold-causing viruses operating in our bolies at any given time, the presumed reason we do not always have a cold is that we have antibodies which keep those viruses from taking command. When we are emotionally strong, those antibodies operate efficiently to keep us disease free.

But if we have not used our anger state to rid ourselves of those conditions which upset us or make us feel inadequate and unworthy, our emotional condition suffers. When we become discouraged, for instance, that discouragement undoubtedly results in an impairment of our emotional state. And that results in our waging a less effective inner fight against germs.

4. *Colitis.* Ulcerative colitis is a condition of the colon which affects thousands of Americans. It can be caused by allergies, but in my experience, it is almost always related to anger expression. When a person either does not use his anger to resolve conflicts or difficulties, or when the use of anger proves ineffective and the conflictual situation remains, one of the most frequently affected physical centers is the colon. I knew one man whose ineffective anger expression obviously contributed to his colitis. He seethed at his domineering wife but never confronted her. When he refused to alter his expressive strategy, his situation became progressively more acute. It was almost as though his body were screaming for him to adopt a new approach.

5. *Hypertension.* During the last fifteen or twenty years, hypertension has become a major medical disorder. A person diagnosed as suffering from hypertension is often highly competitive, restless, and unusually aggressive interpersonally. This is a high-risk patient, unusually vulnerable to coronary attack.

It is well established that ineffectively expressed anger can contribute to physical symptoms. In the next chapter we will consider an interesting theory about how this may occur.

Could It Be That
We Learn to Be Sick?

Most of us, when we were young children, experienced the delights of special attention lavished on us when we were physically ill. We became the center of the household, and first-class service was always forthcoming.

That kind of treatment was undoubtedly reinforcing. It is not difficult to understand why we sometimes got sick almost on purpose.

But it is difficult for a child to lie to a parent about sickness. When the idea of staying home with some ailment evoked expectations significantly more positive than those related to the idea of going to school, and when we wished not to be deceitful, could it be that we learned to be sick? And further, is it possible that some learned that "art" far better than others?

Hold those questions for a minute and consider another line of research.

In 1964 Sandler and Quagliano[2] published a research report about a study they had completed with monkeys. The monkeys were taught to press a lever to avoid being shocked. Af-

[2] J. Sandler and J. Quagliano, "Punishment in a signal avoidance situation." Paper presented at the meeting of the Southeastern Psychological Association, Gatlinburg, Tenn., 1964.

terwards, the pressing of this lever continued to prevent the original shock, but it also produced a lower-magnitude shock of its own. As time went on, the shock produced by their own lever pressing was gradually increased until it was as strong as the one being avoided. And the monkeys continued to press.

Then the avoided shock was discontinued permanently. Now their lever pressing was avoiding nothing. But they didn't quit pressing, even though the shock they were generating was now greater than the one they originally tried so hard to avoid.

This study demonstrates the power of an imagined threat which may no longer exist at all in reality. It also demonstrates the critical point that self-aggression patterns may be acquired because they prove to be an effective way to avoid an even more punishing response from others. The reinforcer of the "get sick" behavior is the tension reduction which is experienced when another's anger is not forthcoming.

If a five-year-old child like Joan Williams were to face a dominating and punishing mother such as she had, and if she were to discover that while her mother did not allow any anger from Joan, her own attitudes did change dramatically when Joan became ill, might that not have reinforced Joan's "get sick" strategy?

And even if that sickness had, over time, become more and more painful to Joan, might she have continued it on the basis of having learned that it successfully blocked her mother's more negative behavior?

And isn't it possible that the illness strategy created its own momentum, so that even though her mother's real threats may have disappeared, Joan's sickness would have continued?

All of this assumes that a person can make herself sick. My experience in psychotherapy has convinced me that this is a valid idea. Some people can make themselves cry by thinking about very sad experiences. Others can make themselves vomit by obsessing over the gruesome details of a picture they've seen or an event they've conjured up. Still others can produce a severe tension headache. So powerful is the human imagination.

These self-generated illnesses may be the result of conscious or unconscious processes. They are often designed to block what is considered to be a less desirable alternative.

But like the monkeys who continued to press the self-punishing lever when all rational justification had vanished, children can become just as "addicted" to getting sick. They have learned to handle anger, but that learning has boomeranged on them.

This unreasonable strategy can be extinguished, and if necessary, persons can be taught far more effective ways of relating to the anger of important figures in their lives.

STRATEGY NUMBER 3—
SELF-PUNISHING

Are you an exploder or a somatizer? If you are either, it must be fairly obvious to you by now. But if you are a self-punisher, you may not be as aware of it. We often beat up on our self-conceptions in quiet and subtle ways, so imperceptibly that sometimes we become aware of it only when we meet up with a crisis in our lives and realize that our self-image is shriveled and drawn.

When Things Go Wrong,
It's Nearly Always My Fault

Mrs. Harrison is a dignified fifty-seven-year-old lady with a soft voice and a gentle manner. She is kind and solicitous in relation to everyone. What I first noticed about her was the way she tried to take care of me. If I was running late when it was time to see her, she would check to see if I needed to make a call or take a break. She was in no hurry.

Beyond being a caring and friendly person, she is obviously well endowed intellectually. But when I first saw her, it was obvious that she was operating at only half speed. She was a fraction of the person she once had been.

She told me about herself in the first few minutes, seemingly because she knew that was what she was to do. She spoke slowly, without much energy, obviously depressed. About six months prior to her coming, her husband had left her for another woman. Although she had tried to cope with the experience—in fact, to see the positive side of it—the bottom seemed to have dropped out of her life.

His announcement had come out of the blue, in a way, and in another way it hadn't. For several months he had been going to the beach to spend weekends on their boat, always coming home late on Sunday night. Although she had missed

him to a degree during these periods, it was also a relief to
have him gone, because she couldn't seem to keep him happy.

But since two weeks after he finally left she had become so
blue that she didn't feel like getting up most mornings. In
fact, she had seriously considered committing suicide, so painful had the experience become for her.

She didn't blame him for leaving, she said. She simply
wasn't much for anyone to want to be around. He was an ec-
centric person, yes, but still she should have been able to
make the marriage a success.

Over time it became obvious that Mrs. Harrison had for
over thirty years denied her hurt and frustration in relation to
Mr. Harrison. She seldom took his gruff manner and provocative actions as seriously as she took her relational deficits.
When things went wrong between them, she almost always
felt guilty and assumed it was her fault. She regularly tore
herself down, and this kept her self-image in tatters.

She was an incredible woman, and she had many accom-
plishments in support of that evaluation. But so successful had
been her vicious attacks on her person that she could only see
herself as a failure. She had started a business with her husband, and she was at least 50 percent responsible for its substantial success. They had raised two outstanding children,
and she had been largely responsible for their parenting.
Moreover, she had managed to maintain close relationships
with a large group of intimate friends, even though her husband was often sullen around them and would fall asleep at
dinner parties.

And she could recognize that her husband, although highly
talented, had treated her as another tool to be used for his
success. He ignored her much of the time—simply took her
contributions for granted.

His insensitivity in relation to others often embarrassed her
in both business and social situations. He was highly unpre-
dictable and unreliable, seldom keeping appointments and
less often following up on promises. As the story unfolded
over the weeks, there was evidence that he was getting back

at his own mother by relating that way to his wife and others.

But Mrs. Harrison wasn't angry about it. In fact, when I eventually mentioned the possibility of her being angry, she was shocked. No one had ever suggested such a thing before. How could she be angry with him when she was the one who had failed? He had only been himself.

It became obvious in time that her well-patterned strategy for dealing with hurt and frustration was to demand more of herself. In effect, she turned her anger toward the inside and set it loose. When her husband left and it became clear that she couldn't control her relationship with him any longer that way, she felt like a miserable failure. And it simply didn't feel comfortable for her to let up on her inner attack.

That inner attack was of course responsible for the eventual depression she experienced and her suicidal thoughts. Mrs. Harrison's inability to express her anger was methodically destroying her own psyche. She had become a frightening enemy—a powerful threat to her own survival.

Turning Anger on Your Psyche

Research indicates that you and I send hundreds of silent messages to ourselves every hour of the day. No one begins to have the power over us that we do.

And for whatever reason, society tends to reinforce us for sending negative messages. To hear your tennis opponent say to himself, "What a lousy shot!" seems reasonable enough. But if he says, "I hit that forehand magnificently!" we might consider that inappropriate.

The same is true in other areas. If your friend looks in the mirror as you go into a restaurant and says, "Boy, am I a mess; that wind's a fright," that's OK. Let her look in that same mirror the next day and say, "I am so pleased with how I look today," and she may have used up her one legitimate self-compliment for the week.

So you can understand how it is so easy for us to get into the habit of delivering angry messages to ourselves. Think how much more legitimate it is in our society to get mad at yourself than it is to get mad at a friend or even a competitor. You are "a most likable person" if you reproach yourself regularly. Some people feel more comfortable and actually enjoy being around self-attackers. The opposite is true of selfcongratulators. They are "conceited," "egotistical," "self-centered"—all very negative labels to lay on persons who may only be trying to be objective about themselves.

And so we produce a high percentage of people who aim their anger inside. Actually, the less an angry self-message is deserved by a person but the more convinced he seems to be about it, the greater his chance of being genuinely appreciated by some persons.

When you're angry, you're aroused. That's what anger means. Maybe you're only a little angry, and so you're only a little aroused. But whenever you're angry, you are more prepared to act than when you have no anger.

So if you've been taught to use that prepared state to go after yourself, you do it with gusto.

We have thousands of self-punishers around. We've taught them to be that way. And every time they do it, we reinforce them some more. By now, for a lot of people, the pattern has become well established.

Depression—A National Epidemic

The *Wall Street Journal* has suggested that our nation is suffering from an epidemic of emotional depression. Many authorities agree that more human suffering has resulted from depression than from any other malady affecting the human race.

There are multiple causes of depression, but two are directly related to the manner in which we handle our anger.

First, since we have observed few effective models in relation to anger expression, we simply don't know how to use our anger constructively. The whole purpose of anger is to prepare us to manage our environment—particularly those parts which cause us to feel hurt, frustrated, or fearful. If we do that poorly, we will regularly experience a sense of inadequacy and helplessness. Our environment will seem unmanageable to us—the problems it presents too difficult to solve.

The second cause follows directly on the first. Discovering ourselves inadequate in relating to external problems, we may then focus additional attention on ourselves and particularly on our failings. Since our society reinforces us so consistently for emphasizing our defects, we become better and better at it.

The end result is that we reduce our self-esteem to dangerous levels. One inner message after another tears at our worth: "I didn't get much done today," "I forgot to take the clothes to the cleaners," "I haven't done a very good job helping Barbie get ready for her party," "I just don't get over to see my parents as much as I should," "I ought to be a better tennis player than I am," "I'm hitting my woods atrociously today."

It doesn't matter that I turned out a massive amount of work yesterday, that I did all the washing, that overall I've been a great mother to Barbie, that I see my parents every week, that I'm one of the better tennis players among my friends, and that I've hit my irons unusually well all day.

I concentrate on what's wrong, what needs improvement, and obviously then, on what's defective. I make myself feel less and less worthy. And that's why my self-concept is like Swiss cheese. I have turned my anger on myself, and I am causing myself to feel depressed. I am inadequate in using anger to deal effectively with the hurts and frustrations of my life, and my consequent tendency to pick on myself is destroying substantial quantities of self-esteem.

Then low self-esteem sets me up for regular defeats, both in relation to the external environment and in relation to my desire to maintain inner balance. The not surprising result of all this is that "epidemic of depression" which haunts so many Americans.

When Life Is Barely Worth the Trouble

Thoughts of suicide are common for persons who feel beaten. And feeling beaten is common for persons who have become their own worst enemies.

We often feel beaten when there is no need to. And once feelings of helplessness get established, they give themselves up with great reluctance.

A fascinating piece of psychological research was reported in 1968 by Seligman.[1] It involved a study of learned helplessness in dogs.

Dogs were placed, one at a time, in a large box which had two compartments separated by a small partition which the dog could easily jump over. One compartment had a metal grill on the floor through which electric shocks could be administered. A light dimmed prior to the giving of a shock, and the dog could avoid the shocks simply by jumping to the other compartment.

Then each dog was placed in a harness so that he could not avoid the shocks. Try as hard as he might, the dog could not

[1] M. E. P. Seligman, S. F. Maier, and J. H. Geer, "Alleviation of learned helplessness in the dog." *Journal of Abnormal Psychology*, 1968, 73, No. 3, 256–62.

escape the compartment rigged with the grill. The light would dim, and he would try to move. But he was held in place, and he had to endure the pain.

The most fascinating finding from this study, among many, was that when the dogs had been given this harness experience for a relatively short time, they no longer seemed motivated to even try to jump to safety. Even after the harness was removed, they did not jump. When the light would dim, the dogs would show multiple signs of anxiety and simply brace for the shock.

This behavior continued seven days later when the dogs were tested again. They did not jump to avoid the shocks.

The experimenters then tried assisting the dogs to the other compartment to demonstrate to the dogs that safety could be easily attained. Still, on subsequent trials the dogs remained rigid in place.

This finding is highly similar to what I have observed with depressed persons who have developed a sense of helplessness in relation to their environment. Their inability to use the power made available to them through the arousal of their anger left them highly vulnerable.

And when they began to further their decline by finding fault with themselves, their sense of helplessness grew even more overpowering.

Handling anger efficiently, as we will see in Section III, can be learned by anyone. Not to learn that skill in this society is equivalent to putting the harness on ourselves and creating an impossible situation when the light dims.

STRATEGY NUMBER 4—
UNDERHANDING

Underhanders are typically the most clever mismanagers of anger. They are like magicians—almost impossible to catch in the act, but somehow they're doing it to you. Many underhanders are unaware of their anger. They think they're just being funny. They argue that they didn't mean a thing by what they said or did. They try to make you think that you're imagining things. But when you feel invisibly punched or cut up or poked at or deflated or put down, trust your feelings. And look around for an underhander.

I Have No Friends Because
No One Ever Calls

Alex Barnes was a forty-two-year-old orthopedic surgeon. His practice was overflowing, but he was tired of it. His three examining rooms were always full, and he saw one case after another all day long with almost no time out. "And I get dozens of time-consuming phone calls everyday," Alex complained. "One night out of every three I'm on call, and it's wild and hectic." His sense of service and the considerable financial remuneration had long before lost their power to motivate him.

Eventually, Alex indicated that he was fed up with his private life too. "My wife and I have almost no sexual involvement. She's never interested. And I feel like a stranger with my kids. My wife makes nearly all the decisions about them, and I'm like an outsider. They talk almost exclusively to her."

When I asked him to name his three closest friends, he couldn't name any. "No one ever calls," he explained. I was stunned by his response. But this made the fact that he had only the most superficial community involvement understandable.

His wife Sandy complained that Alex almost never took initiative in anything. "He sits back in his study and waits for

the kids or me to *consult* him." She seemed bitter. "He wants
the world to come to him and take care of his needs. He never
calls a friend. And he waits for me to take the initiative in sex
and everything else. Then he's never happy with how it goes
and complains that I haven't done it right. I'm tired of failing
with him. And I'm tired of babying him too."

As I listened through the weeks, it seemed obvious that
Alex was destroying himself and everything he touched with
the style of anger mismanagement he had adopted. He always
"attacked" in an indirect way. He did nothing assertive, and
then waited. If you didn't try to move toward him, you had let
him down. And if you did anything to try to meet his needs,
he invariably rated it as "not enough" or "short of the mark."
His was a classic passive-aggressive style. He was angry in the
slipperiest of ways. He never said so, and he always denied it
when asked. He was as hard to get hold of as an eel, but there
was no question about his being very angry.

It was like Alex was getting his only satisfaction from making others feel helpless. And if others got lured into trying to
help him, he worked to defeat them. He was in complete
charge of his cancerous game.

One thing became obvious: He was the only one who could
change his style. And it had to be his idea. He never thought
others' suggestions were worth much. He had to be the one
who decided to stand up and march out of his quagmire.

But this passive-aggressive pattern was so deeply woven
into his personality that there was hardly any area that it
hadn't infected. It seemed to be such a central part of his
identity. How could he ever give it up?

Especially since it was working so well. Designed to be
frustrating to others, it was overwhelmingly successful.

Unfortunately, this was the only way Alex had learned to
express his anger and resentment. That he destroyed his own
happiness in the process of defeating others didn't seem to
matter much. He was a trapped man who wasn't asking for
release.

The Indirect, Underhanded Approach

Can you think of anything that irritates you quite so much as someone who pretends to be the nicest person around but who consistently does you in? It's doubly punishing—she hits you where it hurts the most, but then she claims that she didn't mean to do it at all. And you can't be entirely sure one way or the other. The fact is, she probably can't either.

There are hundreds of indirect ways of expressing anger underhandedly. There are the obvious ones—gossiping, teasing, and obstructing. And the less obvious ones—failing in school, drinking heavily, or having an extramarital affair—all designed to get even with persons who have made you angry. Then there are the people who are consistently late and keep you waiting, and the people who never return your phone calls or answer your letters.

If you look for them, you can find two or three of these indirect expressions every day. As when someone "forgets" to give you an important message; or when you find that your good friend has shared with someone else an item about you which you were sure you had told her in confidence; or when a member of your staff sabotages the team effort in one way or another; or when someone consistently muddles a small group discussion you are trying to lead—or falls asleep in the middle of it; or when a "friend" gives you a check and manages not to have sufficient funds in his account to cover it.

And what can you do? Maybe it *was* an honest mistake. If you confront them, they seem shocked and hurt, act completely innocent, and now appear more wounded than you do.

Some people learn at an early age to express their anger this way. It's usually because they had this approach modeled for them by an important person in their family. Or perhaps because they were prohibited from ever being "really angry," and they happened onto this style quite by accident. It's easy to understand how it got reinforced. People become very attentive when this approach has its way with them the first few times.

But it's a strategy for expressing anger which is virtually never constructive. It is designed not to be. And even though it usually ends up destroying a relationship, it is incredibly difficult to terminate. It's so slippery—for persons on both ends of it. The "actor" is often unaware of his actions. And when he is confronted, there are so many handy cover-up excuses which continually cloud any analysis of what is going on.

Don't Be Obvious, but Get 'em Good

This is the title of the underhander's theme song, I'm convinced. It plays in their heads along the border of their awareness, and it has a catchy melody. How much the underhander listens to the song varies considerably.

I don't think, for instance, that Alex Barnes—the passive-aggressive orthopedic surgeon I talked about before—listened to it much. He often seemed as frustrated with his passive-aggressive style as his wife did. When I would clarify it for him and work with him to develop some new responses to the frustrating experiences of his life, he would try to cooperate—for a while. At least it seemed like he did at the time. Come to think of it, maybe Alex did listen to this song a lot.

But he was "the nicest guy you'd ever want to meet." A lot of people thought so. He was downright charming sometimes. But if you got lured in, you'd had it. He could charm, but from then on you had better be prepared to carry the ball at all times, never to score, and to end up behind by six touchdowns.

There is no getting around the fact that underhanders are by far the most frustrating anger expressers around. The great thing, comparatively, about the exploder is that he gets it over with. If you get beaten up with words or fists, at least you know about it. And after a little while you usually find out why.

But not with the underhander. With him you're never sure about anything, except that it goes on and on. All you do is seethe. You try everything—confront him and he slips away, walk away and he accuses you of not trying, give him your best and it's not good enough.

Judas was an underhander. He lives in history as that disciple of Jesus who did him in. Even though he played a crucial role in bringing about the central event of the Christian story, no one has ever let him off the hook. It was bad enough that he was a betrayer and a traitor. It was even worse that he was underhanded in his approach, thoroughly devious, maddeningly indirect.

Don't you appreciate having people look you right in the eye and taking you on if they're upset with something about you? I think that when people do this, they are set on making solid contact with you in the interests of a constructive resolution.

Underhanders never look you in the eye. They are never that direct. And they aren't interested in constructive endings.

But maybe we shouldn't be too hard on them. They're tragically caught in that style of handling their anger. It can't be working any wonders for them either. What they need is a new song to listen to.

The Sophisticated Pouter—
An Underhanded Giant

You know pouters. They stick out their bottom lip and act sullen. They show their contempt and displeasure that way.

A really sophisticated pouter tries to show contempt without being caught at it. He never does anything as obvious as sticking out his lip.

This kind of pouter has incredible power. When he goes into his act, he can bring an enormous amount of pressure to bear on a group or another person. Without a sound, things start coming apart.

Have you ever been around a person like that?

It doesn't matter where you are—on a tennis court, at the family dining table, at a work situation, or in a college sorority. The sophisticated pouter can perform on any stage under any conditions.

Now if the pouter is fairly new at the game, you might be able to catch him at it. Here are some things to watch for: he is so tight that when everybody else is laughing, he can't for the life of him make his mouth smile. You've got him. Or he becomes even quieter than he wishes to, and he quits participating altogether. And you can pick up a lot of information from his motions too. When he's pouting, his moves are jerky.

Even when he wants to scratch his ear, his arm travels at twice its usual speed.

But when he has become an old hand at pouting, he is almost impossible to catch. You think you know what he's doing, because there's the feeling of punishment in the air. But he tries to make you think you're imagining things. He talks a little bit—not much, but just enough. He smiles too—kind of a dull, "that wasn't very funny" smile. But it covers what he's doing. And his movements are almost exactly the same as they usually are.

But he's doing it to you nonetheless. He's making you feel that this is a pretty dull, unstimulating event. Sometimes he goes after a bigger reward—such as making you feel this is "stupid, poorly conceived, and it's all your fault." And one of his main techniques is to remove his person from you without ever moving his body away.

What he's trying to do is to cause you to feel bad. He wants to make you feel guilty, mostly, for what you've done to him. And then he wants you to take care of him. If he can both punish you and get his way, he hits the jackpot.

And can you believe that this strategy often works—for a while at least?

Let me tell you what I often experience with pouters. Let's say they do it during a tennis game. They suddenly get very silent, no more kidding around, and they don't run very fast after shots or swing very hard. My immediate reaction is to think about what has been going on. Have I done something I need to feel guilty about? If I have, I try to get to the net at the first chance so that I can chat with them and apologize.

But if I sense myself guiltless, I watch awhile longer. And if the person seems not to want to play, I agree to stop. He has usually managed to take most of the fun out of the game anyway.

As we move over to the bench, I might ask if anything is wrong. The pouter never responds to that question in any open way. But if by chance he's not a pouter, he might tell me that he's feeling very sad for some reason that he can't get ahold of, or he's just worn out from an unusually strenuous week. And I can certainly understand both of those states.

But pouters never come straight like that. They're angry, don't want to tell you about it, but definitely want to punish you for it.

Where I get into a lot of conflict is when a pouter is somehow involved in my life, and I don't have much choice about it. Perhaps she's the wife of a close friend—or someone who works where I do. If this person doesn't change, it can make for a very difficult decision about how to handle the matter.

But rest assured of this—pouters are expressing their anger. You can feel it from the second they start. Theirs is a very selfish, immature form of anger expression, and it almost never has any positive consequences.

That's why one thing we can never afford to do with pouters is to reinforce them. To feel bad about ourselves in response to them, or to run to their aid and try to make them feel good, is exactly what they want and exactly the wrong thing for them.

What they need is to be helped to deal with their anger in a much more thoughtful and constructive way. Otherwise, they will almost certainly end up with no one to pout around.

Sarcastic Wit—
The Art of Dart Throwing

"She is hilariously funny, but I always feel uncomfortable around her. Why is that? I know she's not serious when she's going after people that way. She just means it to be funny." One of my clients was working on her relationship with the wife of her husband's partner. And she was having a hard time making "being funny" and "going after people" fit together.

But when some people are funny, it is nearly always at somebody's expense. Sometimes they even make fun of themselves. Can that be hostile?

Yes it can. Verbal aggression dressed up in sarcastic wit, even if aimed at yourself, is designed to jab, maybe penetrate. It's funny, so you really shouldn't take offense at it. But when the laughter dies away, the hot steel points become visible. And the damage is done. It is anger expressed underhandedly.

If the dart is directed at someone else, it's easier to laugh. "I'm sure she would never go after me that way," you tell yourself. But don't bet on it. People with anger to dish out who have learned to camouflage it with a joke seldom discriminate with regard to their targets. They're too eager to score.

Even though they usually take shots at people who aren't present, they can just as easily turn to a more present target.

Anybody is fair game—especially anybody who crosses them or gets in their way.

As I mentioned earlier, some people, even professionals, have theorized that persons who express their anger this way are able to drain an inner pool of aggression and that they become less likely of beating up on someone else in a more serious way.

But research indicates the opposite. Verbal aggression under the guise of wit stimulates further aggression in both the sender and the target. You must know how it feels to be hit. It's hard to laugh, and you think about retaliating.

Who are these "witty" people? Most of them, in my experience, are unusually bright, creative persons. That's how they can be so witty and throw their darts with such precision time after time. But I have found two other qualities in them. They are intensely concerned about how they compare with others, and they do not take the feelings of other people very seriously.

Most of these people are extremely difficult to relate to in any frontal way. They can always say: "Sorry, I was just being funny. I certainly meant no offense." And it won't be long—just long enough for you to turn your back—until they throw some more "funny" darts at you for calling their actions into question.

This underhanded style varies in both the quantity and size of the darts. Some people throw a lot of very small darts, almost invisible, while others throw fewer but larger ones. In both cases persons get hurt—whether they are present to know it or not.

Dart throwers are regularly reinforced by the laughter they generate. And so they keep quipping and punning and picking. But seldom do they realize that their style makes growth in their relationships especially difficult. Remember my client's assessment: "She is hilariously funny, but I feel uncomfortable around her." And relationships characterized by discomfort seldom survive, let alone grow.

Moreover, that dart thrower may well end up being felled by her own self-directed accuracy.

SECTION II

Why Is Anger So Misunderstood?

Learning to Think Straight
About Anger

I want you to be clear about the simple structure of this book.

Section I had to do with the way most people mishandle their anger. I mentioned four basic types: exploders, somatizers, self-punishers, and underhanders. Perhaps you were able to see yourself in the description of one or more of these styles.

Section II is concerned with understanding what anger is exactly; how it is related to hostility, aggression, and hate; and in general, what happens to it under certain conditions. The last part of this section draws on the wisdom of ancient philosophy and biblical teaching to demonstrate an ever-widening consensus.

Section III is designed as a training handbook. The goal is to make you an expert in the handling of your own anger. If you follow the suggestions which are included, I'm convinced you can make substantial progress toward that goal.

With that overall understanding of the book, let's move immediately to Section II.

There are five basic ideas I hope to get across in this section:

1. The capacity for anger is a biological given. We all have it. It is as natural as breathing.

2. Anger *is* physiological arousal. It is being prepared for action. No behavioral component is involved in the definition of anger.

3. When we *do* something with our anger, we have moved to anger expression. And *how* we express our anger is learned. Nothing about it is inherited. Thus, that expression can be modified.

4. There are many ways we can express our anger. Aggression is *one* of those ways. But anger and aggression are independent terms.

5. Anger can be expressed constructively. To choose constructive anger strategies, we must make full use of our capacity to think. When we choose appropriate ways to express our anger, we significantly increase the amount of satisfaction we obtain from living.

Several other subjects will be discussed in Section II. But if you fully understand these five points, you will be well prepared to move to Section III, the training phase.

What Is Anger Anyway?

I've said it before: Every person who has ever lived has experienced anger. The capacity to become angry is an impressive gift which comes as part of our biological inheritance.

Anger is a physical state of readiness. When we are angry, we are prepared to act. Physiologically, what happens is this: More adrenaline is secreted, more sugar is released, our heart beats faster, our blood pressure rises, and the pupils of our eyes open wide. We are highly alert. So when we are angry, all the power of our person is available to us.

This, and this alone, is what anger is. Preparedness. Power.

Notice that I haven't talked yet about what causes this state.

And more importantly, I haven't talked about any behavior related to anger. That is *anger expression*, and it should be thought about independently.

Anger is designed to help us cope with a wide variety of situations. It is a biological mechanism which operates in the interests of survival. If we had no capacity for anger, we would be incapable of asserting ourselves in the world. We would be virtually helpless in the face of countless difficulties. When we learn to use this preparedness effectively, our lives are preserved and enhanced.

So anger is power and preparedness. You are perhaps most powerful and best prepared when you are angry.

That's why anger is dangerous. If all that power is mishandled, it can create all kinds of havoc. People who use anger destructively in relation to others or themselves can do extensive damage.

Important findings from psychological research indicate that how you choose to use your anger is learned. And you can bring it under the control of your thinking and decision making. You can develop the ability to think through how you want to take advantage of all that preparedness. Rather than being relegated to the status of a machine which gets turned on and set loose to run wildly and out of control, you can remain in the driver's seat and direct the action.

What causes your body to become so alert? That's undoubtedly learned too. Your body isn't born with any preprogrammed set to be triggered by certain circumstances.

But at an early age you learn when to set this system in motion. The older you get, the more patterned this learning becomes.

The experiences which most often are associated with this physiological state fall into the general categories of hurt, frustration, and threat. When you find yourself angry, you can often gain considerable information about what is going on in you by asking yourself what you are hurt or frustrated about or what is frightening you.

As soon as you discover the problem you can formulate a strategy for dealing with it. And because of your anger you will have sufficient power available to implement any strategy you select.

One other thing should be said about anger. Because it places you in a high state of readiness, it is physiologically demanding. Thus, when you are angry, you should employ that anger immediately so your body can relax and you can return to the task of relating effectively to the people around you, as well as to yourself. The Bible says: "Let not the sun go down on your anger."

As a matter of fact, if the arousal state is maintained over too long a period, considerable physical damage may result.

Ideally, your body would seldom be activated this way. It would be better if you never needed to be angry. This would substantially reduce the total amount of stress you experience. But once angry, the challenge is to make rapid and effective use of the available resources.

So anger is preparedness and power. It equips us to act decisively in the interests of resolution and healing. It can be brought under our cognitive control, and when it is, we become far more effective in the way we cope with life.

But when anger is set loose to run any course it has been conditioned to run, serious negative consequences can ensue.

That makes the matter of anger expression vitally important to all of us.

How Is Anger Different from Aggression?

I mentioned briefly in Part 2 of the Introduction how anger and aggression are regularly confused by nearly everyone. These two terms must, however, be recognized as independent of one another if each is to be correctly understood.

The term "anger" often has negative connotations in people's minds because it is mistakenly linked with "aggression." Although anger is a powerful, but neutral, inner state of preparedness, some persons assume that, like aggression, it is intrinsically destructive.

Aggression is a behavior, and it is intended to threaten or injure the security or self-esteem of the victim. It means "to go against," "to assault," "to attack." It is a response which aims at inflicting pain or injury on other persons. Whether the damage is caused by words, fists, or weapons, the behavior is virtually always designed to punish. It is frequently accompanied by bitterness, meanness, and ridicule. An aggressive person is often vengeful.

Aggression is one form of anger expression. It is often aimed at forcing compliance with the aggressor's wishes. Sometimes it is intended to be instrumental in the attainment of an objective, while at other times punishment and pain seem its only purpose.

A high percentage of anger expression in our society, and indeed throughout history, has been aggressive. This has contributed to the idea some have that there is no difference between anger and aggression. Thus, anger sometimes has a reputation of being consistently bent on destructive expression. This is very unfortunate.

Let me make my overall evaluation of aggression clear. In my opinion, aggression has long-term negative consequences almost all the time. Even when the use of it produces short-term gains, they are usually canceled out over the long term.

Sometimes clients ask if this aggressive behavior or that one might have positive consequences. For instance, they often ask about spanking or scolding children, or "getting something off your chest" with your spouse.

My answer is that research has demonstrated that aggression seldom produces any long-term gains. My own opinion is that aggressive behaviors between family members, community members, and nations may result in severe negative consequences.

If aggressive behavior is utilized, I recommend that it be kept under the strict control of clear thinking. Before acting aggressively, persons should carefully consider their acts for a long time before implementing them. Since the consequences of aggression are so seldom positive, impulsive expressions of aggression are almost certain to produce negative consequences.

When I see a parent, for instance, become angry and express that anger aggressively by slapping a child, I often predict that the long-term negative results of that behavior will substantially outweigh the positive.

It should be mentioned that there is a significant difference between assertion and aggression. Assertiveness involves the direct expression of one's feelings, needs, or opinions. Aggression is characterized as the delivery of damaging stimuli to another organism. In an excellent book by Alberti and Emmons published in 1974, *Your Perfect Right*,[1] that distinction is referred to: ". . . for aggressive behavior, accomplishment of end goals is usually at the expense of others while for assertive behaviors, neither person is hurt, and unless their goal achievement is mutually exclusive, both may succeed."

Finally, you may wonder why so many people express their anger aggressively. I think it is a simple matter of learning. Aggression is regularly modeled in real life and on television. So the aggressive response is frequently available for copying.

Then because of factors discussed in earlier chapters, that same behavior tends to be consistently reinforced by short-term gratification. Thus, anger expression by means of aggression becomes learned.

But the main point of this chapter is that anger and aggression are significantly different. While anger is a physiological state of preparedness, aggression is but one way it can be expressed.

Anger has great potential for constructiveness. Aggression is seldom a means of expressing anger constructively.

[1] R. E. Alberti and M. L. Emmons, *Your Perfect Right* (San Luis Obispo, Calif.: Impact, 1974).

Even Professionals Have Been Confused About Anger and Aggression

A series of relatively recent research discoveries has led to a quiet revolution in psychological thinking on the subject of anger and aggression.

Some of these findings involve technical matters, and an explanation of them would require more space than we have available. I know of no better review of this body of research than that contained in Albert Bandura's book, *Aggression: A Social Learning Analysis*.[1] But let me briefly sketch the most relevant of the new thinking.

The field of psychology had been dominated for years by the idea that human behavior could be understood primarily in terms of instinctual forces operating from within each individual. Aggressive behavior was thought to be built into the very nature of a person. Biological determinism was a central doctrine used in explaining aggression. Even today, a high percentage of persons continues to believe in something similar—that individuals are innately endowed with an aggressive drive.

This view led to considerable pessimism. If persons were

[1] A. Bandura, *Aggression: A Social Learning Analysis* (Englewood Cliffs, N.J.: Prentice-Hall, 1973).

naturally aggressive, and if that aggression were inevitably expressed in one form or another, the future of the human race seemed in jeopardy. The combination of instinctual aggression, handed down to everyone by heredity, and the rapidly increasing destructiveness of technological tools for aggression left little hope for the future of mankind. But new findings in psychology make decidedly more room for human control in the area of anger expression.

The difference is this: There is increasing agreement that the original idea of man's "natural aggressiveness" is invalid. As a matter of fact, there is overwhelming evidence for a complete departure from the traditional Freudian doctrine that aggression is an inherited destructive drive.

It is undoubtedly true that the neurophysiological mechanisms which give persons the capacity to be both angry *and* aggressive are part of our inherited endowment. Even infants have the neurophysiological equipment to become "angry." At least, we as adults might label an equivalent set of physiological signs in ourselves as "anger."

But there are two important differences in current psychological theorizing. One is that the infant's behavioral expression of this anger state is but random activity—not aggression. If the infant at some later time chooses to behave aggressively, it will be because he learns to do so. Thus, the expression of physiological arousal in the form of aggressive behavior is no longer viewed as innate, but as one of a number of ways this inner state may be learned to be acted out.

I wish to be clear, however, that while the results of psychological studies indicate that aggressive behavior is not the result of inheritance, there is general recognition that physiological arousal—or anger—and aggression have been paired so frequently in our society that aggressive behavior is all too often the "ordinary" way to express anger. And this anger-aggression linkage is fundamentally responsible for the highly tentative world situation, for physical and psychological abuses in the family, for violence in the streets, for a multitude of physical illnesses, and for emotional disturbance of various kinds.

Nonetheless, there has been a dramatic shift in our thinking. There is now considerably more hope about the eventual control which we can obtain in the area of anger expression. Human beings are no longer "condemned" to act in aggressive ways. Society's challenge is to intervene early in a child's development to help her learn constructive ways of expressing her anger. If that "child" is now an adult, and if aggressive behaviors have already been learned, the challenge becomes one of extinguishing the aggression and linking new behaviors with the aroused internal state.

Secondly, the idea of catharsis is no longer held to be valid . . . at least in its earlier form. It was assumed that when a person became angry and was physiologically aroused, some kind of inner drive state developed. Whatever this "drive" actually consisted of in physiological terms, psychologists held that it could be increased by frustration and "drained" by a broad range of aggressive behaviors.

Effective cathartic behaviors were thought to be highly numerous. They could include fantasized aggression, vigorous physical behavior of a general sort which seemed in some way to overlap aggressive behavior, and even watching others aggress.

But current theory in psychology, keying on the contributions of Leonard Berkowitz and Albert Bandura, has changed in a fundamental way. No longer is an internal "aggression drive" which can be increased or decreased considered viable. Only when the aggression succeeds in directly resolving the problem source does the physiological state abate. Otherwise, findings favoring the idea of catharsis are virtually nonexistent. As a matter of fact, study after study has found that behaving aggressively almost always leads to more aggression rather than less. This includes fantasized aggression and watching others aggress.

This has dramatic implications for our life together. It means that aggression which is viewed on television, for example, whether on news programs or detective shows, can actually increase the probability that viewers will act aggressively.

And it means that anger which is expressed aggressively in a therapist's office may actually lead to the reinforcement of aggressive tendencies. "Ventilation therapists" may be unknowingly contributing to a client's aggression problem.

But a number of mental health professionals continue to practice on the basis of the earlier theory.

For instance, in the popular literature of the last ten years there are four or five books which have presented the idea that aggression is a legitimate, and often ideal, form of anger expression. This position is best represented by Theodore Isaac Rubin's highly popular *The Angry Book*[2] and George Bach and Herb Goldberg's *Creative Aggression*.[3] Rubin encourages people to get their anger out. He suggests that "expressing anger reduces anger and makes angry reactions shorter," and further, he encourages his readers to recognize that if they get their anger out and someone else is hurt by what they say: "This is his problem and not yours."

Bach and Goldberg have devised a whole set of creative techniques to help people "let fly" with their anger. These include "the haircut, the insult club, the Virginia Woolf, the bataca fight" and numerous others, all characterized by the opportunity to deliver anger to another person in a highly forceful, aggressive manner.

Fortunately, the new psychology is beginning to develop far more effective techniques for helping persons gain control over the expression of their anger. For instance, a number of experimental studies have suggested that it is possible to teach frustrated nursery school children to express their anger in an entirely constructive way—totally free of aggression.

At the center of this research is a new emphasis on cognitive functioning, a new appreciation of the human capacity

[2] T. I. Rubin, *The Angry Book* (New York: Macmillan, 1969).
[3] G. R. Bach and H. Goldberg, *Creative Aggression* (Garden City, N.Y.: Doubleday, 1974).

for using intellect to gain control over the expression of anger —and, if necessary, to break maladaptive stimulus-response patterns once thought to be permanently established.

Psychology thus recognizes that anger can become a central mechanism for constructive purposes. And so the field as a whole has changed radically. This change is at the heart of the anger management principles which are presented in this book—principles which can be learned by anyone.

How Is Anger Different from Hostility and Hate?

Anger is distinctly different from hostility and hate.

Anger is a state of preparedness. It is a response to specific experiences which trouble us—most often to hurt, frustration, and fear.

As I have pointed out repeatedly, anger is a neutral state in the sense that its power can be used for constructive or destructive purposes.

Hostility, on the other hand, is an attitude. Usually, that person we think of as hostile has developed a generally negative attitude about a number of persons or events.

To encounter a hostile person is like rubbing against barbed wire. You can hardly keep from being ripped in one place or another. They didn't *do* it to you actually—they just *are* that way.

A person who is angry has a substantial amount of power available to deal with their situation. If they are well trained, they will use that power constructively.

But a hostile person is filled with animosity and enmity. They have often become embittered, and their attitude is negative. They are neither prepared for nor interested in constructive action.

A hostile person has not learned to use anger effectively. So he is left with a residue of resentment following every anger transaction. And he often seems pessimistic about his ability to change his life situation.

Hate is hardened hostility. Actually, hate is very much like hostility—hostility which has become progressively more negative in relation to another person, group, or force of any kind.

Here is a way to think of the relationship of the various terms we have discussed:

1. First, we feel hurt, frustration, or fear.
2. As a reaction to these, we become physiologically aroused in order to deal with whatever has hurt, frustrated, or threatened us. This physiological reaction is anger.
3. If our expression of anger over time fails to be effective— that is, if it fails to cope adequately with the hurting (for instance) event—we are left with a residue of resentment. A collection of resentment leads to a generally negative attitude about life. This attitude of negativity and pessimism is referred to as hostility.
4. As hostility hardens, it becomes hate. Hate is usually felt toward that person whom we perceive to be the cause of our own hurt, frustration, or threat, but with whom our anger has been ineffective in producing any change. If we now hate that person, we probably have lost hope of being able to affect any resolution.

So hostility and hate are the result of a long series of ineffective encounters.

What Makes Me Act Aggressively?

Absolutely *nothing* can "make" you act aggressively. When you are aggressive, it is because at your most fundamental level you have chosen to be.

"You can't tell me that there aren't things which *make* me act aggressively," you may be saying. "When someone yells at me or purposely gets in my way, that *makes* me so angry I have to get them for it. Do you mean to tell me that if someone spat in my face, they wouldn't be making me get them back?"

I certainly wouldn't dispute the fact that your way of expressing your anger feels like an automatic response to a number of things which happen periodically in your life. I imagine you could think of fifty events which seem capable of triggering a certain type of anger response from you, so habituated has become that anger response to those events.

But it is crucial for you to recognize that your response to those events and the events themselves are independent. The events may contribute to your distress, but often the interpretations you put on those events and the way you begin talking to yourself about them significantly influence how you feel about them and how you express that feeling. And sometimes those interpretations and internal processes emerge from an irrational belief system. That system needs regular inspection and adjustment.

On the basis of your way of interpreting events, you learned —probably at a very early age—to respond aggressively to certain happenings. And your response was frequently reinforced, at least momentarily.

And you have chosen for so long to continue responding aggressively to those events that your response now seems automatic. And because of this "automaticness" sense, you have come to think of the external event as being in charge of setting off your behavioral sequence.

But it isn't. You are!

In fact, you are so much in charge of your way of being angry that you can substantially modify your response to virtually any external event, however habituated it may have become. And the more you accept the fact that your anger response is governed by your own internal choice, the greater will be your leverage in the modification process. Your habits can be changed, because *you* are in charge—not someone or some event outside of you.

One forty-five-year-old client told me early in therapy that the look his seventy-year-old mother frequently got on her face "just made me furious." Apparently, he would explode like a Roman candle when she looked this way. From his perspective she was in charge of his angry behavior—not him. She pulled the trigger and always had.

When I challenged his assumption, he tried to make me understand. *Her* control of *his* aggression seemed so obvious to him.

He told me about several experiences with his mother. With each new experience he moved back a few years in his life. "When I was about seven," he eventually said, "I wanted to learn how to ski. Every close friend I had was skiing by then, and I was wild to learn. One night at the supper table I asked if I could join a ski class which met at a nearby slope. My friend Hal was in the class, and he and his family had invited me to take the forty-five-minute ride once a week with them. My folks didn't have to do a thing. The lessons were even free. But they said they wanted to think it over.

"The next day I asked my mom about it again. She said they had decided skiing was just too dangerous, and they didn't want me getting hurt . . . so I couldn't go. Her face had that look on it, like it was just too bad what I wanted. That set me off, and I went out of control. I finally walked outside and slammed the door behind me. She came out a little later and said that she would talk to my dad about it again." It worked.

Sadly, this man at forty-five was still going out of control with his mother when she got that "certain look on her face." He had learned to explode this way when he was young. And he had discovered that this wild response worked with her. She unknowingly reinforced him when he "lost control." So through the years, he did it more and more often. And before long it became virtually automatic—so automatic that he had come to think of it as totally out of his control. *She* made him act this way.

As therapy progressed he concluded that however great the gains were that he experienced from getting anger off his chest at his mother, the costs were substantially higher. He began to work on thinking of his response to his mother as a function of his *own* choice. Like Gary Sheridan, the baseball player we discussed earlier, this client engaged in a series of carefully designed exercises.

And he soon extinguished that primitive pattern. His mother could set her face in any way she wished, but he could choose what his response would be. He felt like a released man. She wasn't able to *make* him angry. He was in charge. And he could select a strategy for dealing effectively with his mother.

Nobody can make you behave in any way. You choose how to use your anger. And it makes a huge difference when you fully realize this.

Why Do I Choose to Explode Sometimes?

Now that's the way the question should be phrased. And it's a crucial question which every person needs to answer for himself.

There is a significant difference between ideal answers to this question and the answers most of us would have to give if we told the truth.

I suspect that we often choose to explode for absolutely idiotic reasons. It might pummel our pride, but it would be a good exercise to tell another person exactly why we chose to be angry the way we did after each anger episode. "I just thought I could get my way if I exploded at her." "I became impatient with trying to 'relate it through,' so I decided to get worked up and throw a tantrum." "I felt so frustrated and helpless, and I knew I would feel a lot more in charge if I got angry." "I recognized that he was right, but I didn't want to give in—so I coiled myself and struck."

This kind of explosive anger is almost always expressed in the form of aggression, and it leads to highly charged chaos and inevitable deterioration.

But that certainly doesn't mean that there aren't times when the experience of anger is vital to the process of living.

Remember that anger is preparedness. And it makes sense to be prepared when you have an important job to do. You have an important job to do when in relation to a certain external or internal event you are experiencing feelings of pain. Your job is to relate to that event effectively enough that you don't have to feel the pain any longer—so that you become totally free of it.

For instance, imagine that your spouse or closest friend totally misunderstands you. And because of that misunderstanding he distances himself and refuses to relate meaningfully to you. You are experiencing a deep sense of frustration and a considerable amount of hurt. You become angry, and your anger is crucial to the healing of your relationship.

But you have a choice about how to express that anger. You can yell at him, pout, throw things, or pretend that you're feeling nothing—but then tighten up your neck in search of a headache. Or you can sit down and work out a strategy designed to resolve the misunderstanding and heal the hurt.

Assuming you know how to use that anger effectively—and that is a key assumption—this is certainly an appropriate time to be angry. Your intimate relationship is in trouble—and it needs help.

Anger can be a constructive response to almost all internal and external events in relation to which you experience hurt, frustration, or fear. The variety of events which fall into these general categories are numberless. That's why learning to use anger profitably can be such a benefit.

For instance, you undoubtedly experience hurt feelings fairly frequently in response to all sorts of internal and external events. Take criticism for example. At the base of most criticism and attack is a process of evaluation—the evaluation of you as a person. When someone is evaluating you, they are holding their standard up to you and comparing your quality with their standard. If you fall short, you are treated with less respect. That hurts. Assuming you agree with the process and the verdict, you feel doubly humiliated and hurt.

You are angry. OK, use that anger to cope with the hurt. If you didn't feel anger, you would have little capacity for therapeutic response. And there is no way that you want to just sit there forever feeling hurt. Your goal is immediately clear: to relate to the hurt so effectively that you eliminate it. There are numerous routes to that objective. Most likely, given the evidence, you will work on yourself—your expectations and/or your behavior.

It also makes good sense to choose to be angry when frustration is your inner experience. Frustration is usually a response to being thwarted in moving toward a goal or objective. When you can't do what you seek to do or you can't be what you seek to be (for example, understood, appreciated, or cared for), you experience frustration. Anger used wisely can result in the reduction or even elimination of the frustration. You still may not be able to reach your objective, but you may be able to modify your goal or exert patience in relation to your timing. There are numerous ways to resolve frustration. But they all require high levels of concentration. And that's where anger becomes crucial.

Finally, anger is often effective in relation to experiences of fear. Fear is usually our response when something or someone we hold dear is threatened. When our self-esteem, physical safety, loved one, or our community are threatened, we become afraid.

When we become angry, we are prepared to encounter these threats in an effort to dissolve them. We refuse to become paralyzed by our fear. We relate to the source of that fear in a positive and constructive way.

Why am I angry sometimes? Because I need to be prepared to cope effectively with my life. What parts of my life can I cope with most effectively through the expression of my anger? Those in relation to which I experience hurt, frustration, and fear. And what is the ultimate objective of my anger expression? The management of those internal and external sources of hurt, frustration, and threat so that my inner pain may be kept to an absolute minimum.

Do I Have to Tell People
When I'm Angry with Them?

When you are angry, it is almost always because you are experiencing some form of pain. And as you experience that anger, your overarching objective can be brief and straightforward: to relate so effectively to your pain source that you need feel no further pain. This objective will guide your strategizing about every detail connected with how you express your anger.

So whether you tell one or more persons that you're angry with them will depend entirely on how you decide to cope with your pain. Certainly, there are no hard-and-fast rules. I can think of some reasons you might want to share your anger at times. And I can easily imagine your not choosing to verbalize it at other times.

Some psychologists and psychiatrists have a consistent bias toward "telling." When their patient is angry in relation to someone else, these professionals immediately encourage them to share that feeling. They would argue that the verbalizing of anger releases a person and makes him feel less trapped in his pain. So these helpers use expressions such as: "Get it off your chest" and "Clear the air."

Moreover, they would hold that telling others when you are

angry with them at least alerts them to your reaction. It gives them feedback which they may need to determine how they can most effectively relate to you. And if you tell them in a way that invites their participation in dealing with the underlying problem, you have perhaps obtained considerable help in attaining your ultimate objective.

Language is a tremendous gift. It allows us to communicate our most sensitive feelings in a way that no other skill makes possible. If we use language well, our anger can often be expressed constructively even under highly stressful circumstances.

Two additional arguments can be advanced in support of this position. When you share your anger, at the very least you get some kind of process in motion. And you eliminate the three risks which exist when you fail to use your anger at all: (1) That you will let your anger out in an underhanded way that will have little positive effect; (2) That you will take it out on your body; (3) That you will attack yourself and deplete your self-esteem supply.

But there are plenty of reasons not to share your anger at times too. Many psychotherapists are concerned about the negative consequences of doing so.

For one thing, it is very difficult to talk about your anger toward other persons without threatening them. It takes tremendous skill for you to tell a person that you are angry without their thinking that you are blaming them for what you think is wrong. If the latter is their perception, even if you're not blaming, their reaction may be to defend—and that defensiveness may only escalate the problem.

There are other reasons you might decide not to verbalize your anger directly. One is that it's sometimes too easy to tell someone you're angry with them. It leads to a kind of superficial process, and neither of you talks about the real problem about which you are angry. If you don't proceed to that deeper work, nothing has been gained. In fact, you may have wasted the resources which could have provided progress in time.

I have found that people who are eager to tell others of their anger are frequently looking for superficial solutions. They often want to shortcut what is necessary—what may be a very difficult, even wrenching, process. And sometimes they trick themselves into thinking they have completed their task when they communicate their anger. Actually, they have barely begun.

But as useful as all these considerations are, they miss the essential point in a way. That is this: *You* are the one in charge of your anger and how you express it. *You* need to know every aspect about what you are experiencing and why.

Then *you* develop a strategy for resolving the difficulty about which you are angry. Your strategy will take hundreds of details into consideration.

And if that strategy includes telling another that you are angry with her, fine. But your strategy may involve attacking the problem in a totally different way that will call for keeping your anger a secret.

After all, it is *your* anger. And you are in charge of using it effectively—to solve your problem, to end your pain, to get you back on the track again, to make things right.

You don't have to tell anyone. But under certain circumstances, for good reasons, you may often choose to.

Should I Feel Ashamed
About Being Angry?

Marsha was thirty-two, shy, but unusually beautiful. Her husband was a highly successful international trader from Brazil. They had been married for about five years—happily for the first three, but less so recently since his mother came to live with them. Marsha felt totally incapable of handling this strong, dominating woman who made so many demands on her son, Marsha's husband, and on Marsha herself.

"I feel overmatched around her," Marsha said. "My husband says I have to stand up to her, let her know she can't control me, hold my ground, but the only time I can do that is when I'm angry. And I always end up feeling ashamed of myself after I've let my anger show. Like, what kind of person am I anyway—getting angry like this?"

Marsha is representative of dozens of persons I've seen who feel ashamed about being angry. In our culture there seems to be an unwritten rule that being angry is inappropriate—a little like walking down Main Street at noon in only your pajamas. As pervasive as that rule seems to be, both now and historically, I have found it to be poorly thought through and generally misunderstood.

To feel anger is perfectly natural. The capacity for experiencing this emotion is an essential part of our biological inheritance. If you could feel no anger, you would be incapable of relating effectively to the sources of pain you inevitably encounter.

So rather than feeling ashamed about being angry, it would be better to take the anger for granted and get about the task it prepares you so effectively to accomplish.

But the reason most people experience embarrassment in connection with anger has to do with anger expression. When a persons says, "I got angry with him," they may actually mean that they experienced anger and expressed it to him aggressively. Maybe they yelled at him, used degrading words, acted explosively. And now they are embarrassed—not about being angry, although they sum it up that way, but actually about the way they handled that anger.

Someone else may be embarrassed about having expressed anger underhandedly—with sarcasm, pouting, or back-stabbing. Still other persons may be embarrassed about their ulcers or their depression.

And to the degree that you have expressed your anger destructively, it's appropriate to be embarrassed. Especially if that embarrassment leads to a re-evaluation of your strategy for expressing yourself.

There's one other aspect of anger which may legitimately cause embarrassment. It has to do with what you get angry about. For instance, if you find that an excessive number of life situations are threatening to you and you get angry about them, you may need to work on your self-concept. You must be viewing yourself as unusually fragile and easily hurt. It may be that you are basing your self-worth on a flimsy foundation. If you are, you can change that.

Or if you find yourself continually frustrated and angry, you may well need to adjust your goals or develop greater discipline and productivity in reaching the goals you have already established for yourself.

If your frequent "attacks" of anger are embarrassing to you, and if that embarrassment leads you to struggle with your view of yourself or wrestle with your goals and objectives, then embarrassment may be a very constructive feeling for you to have.

So the capacity to experience anger is a gift of great value, and embarrassment about being angry periodically is inappropriate. But when anger is expressed destructively, embarrassment may serve an important function. Especially if it causes persons to reflect on themselves.

And when frequent anger reveals significant underlying problems relating to the way you view yourself, the pain of embarrassment may motivate the action necessary to shore up your self-system.

How Do You Know You're Right About Anger?

If you were sitting here with me right now, I can imagine that you might want to ask me some questions about all these ideas I've presented to you. And the main question on your mind might be: "How do you know you're right about anger?" Let me tell you what I'd say if you were sitting here.

I think I'm right for three reasons. The first has to do with my personal experience.

As I mentioned early on, anger is an emotion I've had a hard time taming in my own life. Learning how to make anger a significant ally in my pursuit of the abundant life was for years a confusing and frustrating struggle.

The person who influenced me most from junior high on was a friend of mine, a boy who was growing up in a family much like my own. His father was a powerful man, a prominent leader in our town, and his modeling for his son and his son's modeling for me contributed significantly to many parts of our lives, but in particular, to the way the two of us handled our anger.

As I look back on us, we largely mishandled our anger in at least two ways. We usually employed the underhanded, indirect approach, but periodically, we exploded.

Our underhandedness was well developed—sarcasm was our specialty, but no indirect form of expression was unexplored by us. We drove our cars fast and dangerously. We played every kind of prank we could think to play. We were expressing our anger without ever knowing it.

Our explosions were designed to shortcut more demanding but obviously necessary ways of handling our feelings. And unfortunately, we were too often reinforced. One of the hardest lessons I've had to learn is that point I have repeatedly mentioned—short-term gains are almost always insignificant compared to the corresponding long-term losses.

But now I know the consequences that disciplined effort in this area can have.

So I think I'm right about anger because of what I've experienced personally.

But by far the largest percentage of my experience with anger has come from years of clinical practice. I have talked intimately with several hundred people.

What I have become confident of is that most persons are, at best, thoroughly confused about anger. They often think it is inappropriate to be angry at all. They are unaware of any difference between anger and aggression. They have almost never distinguished between anger and hostility. Anger remains for them a largely unexplored subject, one which causes frustration and feelings of hopelessness.

Most persons I've seen have, over the course of their lives, adopted self-defeating styles of expressing their anger. They are exploders, somatizers, self-punishers or underhanders. They've never been helped to recognize that anger expression is learned and therefore modifiable. They assume their anger patterns are genetically fixed. That anger might become a significant ally in constructive living has never crossed their minds.

No person I have known as a client or an acquaintance has ever worked—previous to our working together—on developing expertise in the area of anger expression, at least as far as I have known.

But persons who have followed a carefully worked out plan for developing their capacity in this area make progress. Their growth does not all take place overnight, or easily. It takes time and hard work, but that kind of effort inevitably pays off.

Beyond my own personal experience and the experience I have had in clinical work, I think I'm right about anger because of what I've read in philosophy, the Bible, and contemporary psychology. Before we move to Section III, let me share the results of that reading with you.

The Wisdom of Ancient Philosophy

Anger has been a subject of intense interest throughout recorded history. I was surprised to discover that Greek and Roman philosophers had so thoroughly analyzed anger and so carefully detailed their findings.

Surprisingly too, the careful and systematic treatment of anger and aggression in these early writings is fresh and alive. Many of the conclusions contained in them remain highly relevant to a twentieth-century consideration of the subject.

Solomon Schimmel[1] has carefully traced the contributions of three prominent philosophers: Aristotle (4th century B.C.), Seneca (1st century A.D.), and Plutarch (2nd century A.D.). His important article, containing a generous number of pertinent quotations, is a gold mine for any person especially interested in philosophy's contribution to this subject.

These philosophers wrote extensively about the dangers inherent in anger. They recognized that people had not been trained to deal with the awesome power which anger makes available. They shuddered as we do about the way anger is so easily mishandled—for example, expressed as aggression in the

[1] S. Schimmel, "Anger and its control in Graeco-Roman and modern psychology." *Psychiatry*, 1979, 42, 320–37.

form of violence and punishment. They wrote dramatically about all the destruction wrought by "anger-fuelled aggression." They argued persuasively for the total separation of anger and aggression.

Secondly, they totally believed in the power of reason to maintain control over the passions. What I have referred to in an earlier section as "the importance of cognitive functioning" was central to their strategizing.

Thirdly, their major interest was to assist their readers in developing self-control when angry. They were committed to the idea that styles of expressing anger can be modified. And they developed a number of training techniques for building control. Many of these techniques have not been improved upon to this day. Some of them will be described in Section III.

Finally, they stressed the necessity of maintaining a highly disciplined, long-term training program in anger management —and they suggested that such a program should include continual review, repeated practice sessions, and "deep assimilation." They stressed that anger outbreaks can be so sudden that persons must be constantly vigilant.

These ancient philosophers were well acquainted with anger's power and its potential for destructiveness. But they were equally convinced that anger-expression styles are a function of learning and that they can be modified in significant ways.

The Teaching of the Bible Regarding Anger

The Judeo-Christian faith is of vital importance to a high percentage of Americans. The source of authority within that movement is the Bible—both the Old and New testaments. Since these writings are fundamentally influential for a high proportion of persons within American society, their importance is difficult to overestimate for the culture as a whole.

When analyzing biblical teaching regarding anger, a fundamental misunderstanding is virtually inevitable apart from recognizing that biblical writers, when writing about strictly human anger, did not often distinguish between anger and aggression. They assumed in most cases that anger included an aggressive behavioral component.

Anger is a commonly reported occurrence in Judeo-Christian history. God is reported as being angry several hundred times in the Old Testament alone. Jesus was regularly angry in relation to those who opposed him and toward his own disciples. Leading figures throughout biblical history—prophets, kings, and other designated leaders—frequently are described as angry. When Moses, for example, came down from the mountain and found the Israelites forming a golden calf to worship, the Bible says that he threw down the stone tablets which contained the law, and his anger "waxed hot."

But biblical writings view anger as extremely dangerous. While the Bible clearly teaches that human beings can choose how they will express feelings of anger, there is a strong emphasis on the almost inevitable linkage between anger and aggression. In the Wisdom literature of the Old Testament (Job, Psalms, Proverbs, and Ecclesiastes), where the subject of anger gets its fullest treatment, and throughout nearly all of the New Testament, anger is assessed as "dangerous" and as having "evil consequences." Some passages contain an expressed warning to "put anger away"—even what some might think of as justifiable anger. The Bible regularly honors the long-suffering person and refers to her as wise, but speaks of the angry person as foolish. The judgment of the New Testament, apart from two passages, is that anger is too often expressed destructively by humans.

There is no question but what the Bible is overwhelmingly negative about any anger expression which involves aggression. And because so much anger is expressed aggressively, the Bible takes great pains to warn its readers about anger's likely consequences.

But to leave our understanding of biblical teaching on anger at this point would ignore additional important data. Consider these points:

Anger is recognized as a biological given. The very Hebrew words which are translated "to be angry" literally mean "to snort" and "to be hot or passionate." Anger has a distinctly physical quality about it, and the capacity for anger is present in everyone.

If all anger were prohibited, it would mean an enormous loss of the very passion which is fundamentally characteristic of the Judeo-Christian faith. In fact, the critical thrust of the Bible is the passion of God, born at the center of his disappointment and wrath in response to man's continual breaking of the covenant, and which culminated in the sending of "His only begotten Son" to re-establish His relationship with hu-

SECTION III

A Training Manual

How to Be an Expert
in Handling Your Anger

There are few experiences in life quite so exciting as knowing that you have become an expert in handling your own anger. If you have often felt yourself a hostage to your temper, expertise as an anger-energized problem solver has to be a supremely attractive goal. Or if the effects of indirectly expressed—but maybe unrecognized—anger have destroyed valued relationships of yours, caused you to experience physical pain, or left you with a negative self-concept, I don't have to remind you of how nice it will be to take full control over this part of your life.

I want to be clear about this: *Every* person can master his or her own anger. If you are an exploder, you can break that destructive habit. If you have directed your anger at your own body, you can stop that. If you have aimed your anger at your self-concept, that can change. And if you have expressed your anger in an indirect, underhanded way, that doesn't have to be the case any more. Any person can develop constructive ways of expressing their anger while extinguishing destructive old patterns.

But I cannot minimize the hard work it takes. Don't expect to read this book and suddenly be a different person. You'll know *how* to be a different person when you finish this book, but becoming one will require a maximum effort. I mean your *finest* effort! I'll tell you how to do it—what to look for, how to get started, where to spend your time—but you're the one who will have to do the work and exert the discipline.

In the place of anger that gets you in trouble, you can learn to use anger to get your problems solved. Anger you once used to beat up on your kids or on the inside of your own body can be used to remove the boulders in your path, the barriers between you and joyful living.

It will require a balanced effort. You'll see what I mean as you read on. You'll need to get your self-concept in good shape. And you'll need to become clear about your anger values. Then staying in close touch with your feelings will be essential. . . . But we're getting ahead of ourselves.

Becoming an expert on anything is not easy. But there's nothing like it for a deep sense of inner satisfaction. And being an expert on your own anger is an exceptional prize, one worth almost any effort.

ANGER MANAGEMENT PRINCIPLE NUMBER 1

The Ultimate Answer: A Solid Self-concept

Violations to self-esteem through *insult* and *humiliation* are perhaps the most powerful elicitors of anger that we know about. When your potency and status are threatened, you will almost automatically become angry.

So the first thing we have to do if you're going to be an expert in handling your own anger is to get your self-concept into shape. When it comes to taking charge of your life, literally nothing is as important as a solidly constructed self-system.

There are at least two reasons for that. (1) When your self-concept is well put together and your self-esteem supply is plentiful, you have ample energy to run your life. When problems develop and you become angry, you are prepared to use those resources to think your problems through and move decisively against them. And (2) Because you feel positively about yourself, fewer experiences will seem frustrating, threatening, or hurtful to you. You will more easily manage those experiences which might, under less positive conditions, present trouble.

Obviously, it's at least a two-way street. The more positively you view yourself, the less anger you experience. And the more effectively you handle your anger, the better you will feel about yourself. I say "at least a two-way street" because you can take it one step further: The better you feel about yourself, the more effectively you will process your anger. As a matter of fact, the ability to handle large quantities of anger in a constructive way is one criterion of a strong self.

That's the beauty of working on both your self-concept *and* your anger expertise at the same time. Any improvement in one immediately benefits the other. And when you get both of these systems moving at once, the momentum you can build leads to incredible growth. That's what I want for you.

So now the focus is on you—on your strengths and attributes. The goal is for you to view yourself in increasingly positive ways. What we know for a fact is that the stronger your self-concept becomes, the easier it will be to manage your anger. We're on the way.

The Critical Dynamic:
Unconditional Love

Your self-esteem depends on your getting loved—loved with unconditional love. I can be more precise. The degree to which you get loved unconditionally will *determine* your level of self-esteem. Unconditional love is absolutely critical.

But what is it actually? Where do you get it? How do you know when you have it? And how does it work?

Unconditional love has two fundamental qualities: (1) It is given without regard for the objective value of the person or thing which is loved; and (2) It is given without any strings or conditions attached. In both of these cases mutuality and reciprocity are ignored criteria. Whether the other person can give something in return which is of comparable value is not even considered.

That's the kind of love which can turn your life around and raise your self-esteem level to new heights. When you find love like that, you are set free to become that person you were meant to be in all your uniqueness. And when you experience yourself in the middle of that kind of freedom, you can't help feeling good about who you find yourself to be.

Where do you get love like this? Let's face it—this kind of love is a scarce commodity, because this is a world which teaches us to negotiate with love. "I'll love you if you'll love me." "I'll be your friend if you'll be mine." "I'll care for you as long as you meet my conditions." These are more like business arrangements—negotiated deals.

The thing that's wrong with this kind of love is that you have to *earn* it. It may well require that you violate your true self in order to get it. "I'll love you as long as you don't cry—as long as you're a good baby." "I'll love you as long as you get good grades in school." "I'll love you as long as you are a strong person and a good provider." "I'll love you as long as you are beautiful, as long as you meet my needs, as long as you keep the house clean, *as long as . . .*" That's the kind of love we're used to.

But we want to be loved *for no good reason at all.* We want to be loved not because we meet conditions, but just because of our uniqueness. And we want to be free to become who we really are without having to fear that we might lose that powerful love which seems so crucial to us.

Where do you find *this* kind of love? Carl Rogers, one of America's most distinguished psychologists, says this love—which he calls "unconditional positive regard" or "nonpossessive warmth"—is essential to the process of personality change. And he suggests that within the psychotherapy relationship the effective therapist can provide this kind of love.

And there are moments when it seems like we get loved this way by others too—parents, friends, lovers, children. The problem is that we can never be sure that if we ceased meeting the unidentified conditions of these persons we would still be loved.

We all scramble after this kind of love in our own ways and our own places.

When I was in graduate school, a professor I deeply respected observed that the central tenet of the Christian faith revolves about the idea of unconditional love. He talked about the Greek word "agape," and he pointed out that the Christian good news is that every person is loved unconditionally. He maintained that Jesus gave his life to weave into the fabric of existence a new truth—the truth that in reality itself every person is loved without conditions. I came to believe this, and ever since I've been about the task of trying to assimilate what this means for me.

I find it agonizingly hard to break away from trying to earn love. The principle I learned in school and the "real world" is that "you get what you earn, and what you earn is what you're worth." Beyond having internalized that mostly unspoken principle, I have found there is something independence-producing about earning love for yourself. If you could once master it, ultimately you wouldn't need anybody.

But what I found is that as long as I was trying to earn love, I had to meet other people's conditions. Essentially, that put others in charge of running my life. And I was getting further and further away from being my authentic self. I was never free just to sit back and be me. And until I could be just me, I could never experience much self-esteem.

How do you know when you find this kind of love? When you suddenly sense that there is nothing you could do or be that would ever separate you from the love another has for you, you know you're loved unconditionally.

And how does this love work? What happens, I think, is that unconditional love sets you free from what Rogers calls "conditions of worth." You no longer have to be anything in particular in order to be loved. You can begin the journey toward self-discovery with no preset destination. In each moment you can simply be authentically yourself.

So there's the chain. Anger expertise requires a strong and positive sense of self. A strong sense of self requires unconditional love which sets you free to engage in self-discovery.

Wherever you can find this kind of love, embrace it. Get in the way of it. Sacrifice everything for it. It will make possible the most magnificent experience life offers you—the personal realization of who you are.

And it will contribute more than anything else to your becoming a master of your own anger.

And People Who Make You Feel Good About Yourself

The people with whom you associate will have a substantial effect on your self-esteem. The secret is to be surrounded with persons who have that delightful knack of helping you feel good about yourself.

The world is full of "judges." These are people who set themselves up to evaluate you—how you look, how well you produce, how moral you are, how witty you seem.

And they like you *if* you meet their conditions. If you fail to dress the way they think you should or behave according to their standards, they withhold their approval of you.

So you're always on trial. Sometimes you come out OK— other times you don't. But invariably, in the presence of these people your self-esteem fluctuates around its lowest point.

Obviously, if you have a choice, stay away from conditional givers, judges, evaluators—especially if their opinion seems crucial to you.

You want to be around people who genuinely seem to care for you without conditions. They know how to set you free to be yourself. Your anxiety level drops dramatically around them because you're not on trial.

There's an organization in America called Young Life. Several thousand Young Life persons work with high school students. All three of our daughters, when they were in high school, were deeply influenced by Young Life workers. I know why. When these staff members came around our home, I got the same feeling our daughters did. They seemed to care for me—genuinely. When they asked me how I was, they actually seemed interested in my answer. They knew how to listen—and they listened a lot.

These people had a simple gift to give. It centered around unconditional positive regard. And I watched that simple gift change dozens of lives.

I personally like to associate with individuals who make two valuable contributions to my life. They set me free by communicating unconditional acceptance. And then, totally independent of that acceptance, they expect excellence from me. They encourage me to actualize my full potential, be my best self, produce my finest product. But whether I do or not seems irrelevant to how they feel about me.

People who can relate to you like that are of infinite value. Their value is closely linked with their own internal strength and health. They are obviously free themselves. Somewhere along the line they must have experienced a healthy dose of unconditional love. And they were so changed by it that they don't need to place conditions on their acceptance of others.

What I would like you to do right now is to think about all the people in your life—friends, family members, fellow employees, boss, neighbors. Make a careful list—probably a very short one—of those people who have that quality of being able to offer unconditional love like I've described.

Once your list is complete, make sure you spend plenty of time around these people from now on. Don't fail to make them a regular part of your life. And when you're with them, settle back in the luxury of the freedom you experience in their presence.

And a Close Friendship
with Yourself

No friendship you have is as crucial to your self-esteem as that friendship you maintain with yourself. In fact, all your other friendships combined are not as important to the way you feel about yourself as your internal friendship with you is.

In support of this radical statement, consider the thousands of messages you send every day to your own self-assessment center. The content of these messages undoubtedly determines the way you evaluate your worth. And the evaluation you make of your worth invariably sets your self-esteem level.

If you encounter unconditional positive regard in your relationship with a friend, it will contribute significantly to your self-esteem. But because that person has so much less opportunity to affect you than you do—that is, he can transmit so many fewer messages to your assessment center—the value of his unconditional regard will ultimately depend on the degree to which you buy into what he is saying and begin sending the same message.

If you continue sending negative evaluations about yourself, the sheer quantity of your messages will easily drown out your friend's unconditional message. The obvious goal is for you to become the source of the unconditional message. When that happens the leverage you enjoy from your "inside" position will make enormous change possible in an incredibly short period of time.

Most persons I encounter engage in continual self-evaluation. "I look good today," or "I look bad." "My hair is too long, and I just couldn't do anything with it." "I'm running late again—as usual." "I don't think I'm being very interesting." By the thousands these messages flash across the brain.

Unfortunately, most people spend considerably more time focusing on their faults than on their strengths. They assume that's their responsibility. If something about them is good—or even OK—they don't have to think about it anymore. Now they can give more thought to what needs attention—to what is wrong.

But there is a serious potential danger here. For in the process of attending to their defects these people are establishing an image of themselves in their own heads. And defect finding leads as sure as anything to "I am defective." And "I am defective" leads to "I'm not worth much." And two or three doses of "I'm not worth much" is all it takes to knock self-esteem down a notch or two.

But the reversing of that trend will create exactly the self-image you wish. Spending time emphasizing your strengths, congratulating yourself every chance you get, and becoming your personal cheerleader—that kind of self-reinforcement can have tremendous value.

For example, when you begin to recognize your own progress in learning to use your anger constructively and to pat yourself on the back for your hard work and obvious success, you will be engaging in a very friendly act.

I assume you need a *close* friend, and you need that close friend to be you. The most effective way I can think of to get that friendship started is to sit down right now and draw up a list of your attributes. Put every item on that list you can think of. Focus on your body, your mind, your personality, your character, your social self—consider all the parts of you.

And when you finish your list, read it over and reflect on it.

It will be most helpful if you read it aloud to yourself at least once a day every day this week.

But in the final analysis your appreciation of yourself will not depend on the length of your list of positive attributes. Rather, it will be due to your having been created unique and loveable. The fact is, that no one in history can replace you. And the clear word from the Bible is that you are enormously worthy solely on the basis of the magnificence of the created you.

This positive message about your worth needs to be transmitted repeatedly to your brain. It will prove decisive in your efforts to build self-esteem. As you gain a deeper and deeper sense of your essential worth, you will be able to grow in self-esteem. And your self-conception will include an objective assessment of your strengths and weaknesses. This assessment will, of course, have nothing to do with your sense of worth. That worth is totally secure simply on the basis of the fact of your being—that part of creation which is you.

ANGER MANAGEMENT PRINCIPLE NUMBER 2

Organizing Your Anger-Aggression Values

As crucial as unconditional love is, destructive anger patterns often resist change even after a person's self-concept has become significantly more positive. The redirection of individual patterns of anger expression requires additional skills which can be developed by those who commit themselves to the task of learning them.

In my work with people who mismanage their anger, one conclusion has become well established. Those who wish to develop expertise as an "anger specialist" must begin their training well in advance of any anger episode. Learning to express anger constructively requires careful preparation under conditions which allow for clear and systematic thinking.

If you wait until the angry moment to begin your mastery efforts, you may express your anger in habituated behavior sequences before you know what has happened. If you are an exploder, you may say or do something automatically without even thinking about it. If you are a somatizer, your conscious denial of anger and immediate physical change may happen faster than you can imagine. And so on.

So what you must be sure of is that you become angry only

after you have given plenty of thought to every aspect of how you're going to handle it. You need to be completely prepared for every emergency.

That means you must know exactly where you stand on the important issues involving anger. And more than that, you must have considered your stance so carefully and so often that you have strong conviction behind you. Then you will be ready to move quickly and decisively when the anger arises. That is what it takes to extinguish old anger-expression patterns and build new, constructive ones.

I assume all of us are especially interested in our own happiness. We seek a maximum amount of pleasure and a minimum amount of pain. Moreover, we are eager to enjoy intimate relationships with a few persons, and we wish to contribute to the larger society and receive its general approval. We essentially desire to behave in ways which will result in long-term benefit to ourselves, our intimates, and humanity as a whole.

From my vantage point, then, the most crucial "anger issues" require especially well-developed answers by you well in advance of "game day."

Question Number 1

Do I enjoy getting angry?

Plenty of people do, of course. They feel energized and powerful when they're angry as at no other time.

Your answer to this question will make a significant difference on those occasions when a little manipulation one way or the other by you will determine whether you become angry or not.

Question Number 2

When I am angry, do I want to be in full control of my behavior, or spontaneous?

In other words, do I want to decide what I do with my anger, or do I want to ride it out the way a surfer rides a wave?

Question Number 3
  If I want to be in full control, am I willing to spend the energy which is required to stay ahead of the action?

  This question is vitally important, because full control requires the kind of vigilance athletes maintain on the day of a game. But in the case of anger, you seldom know ahead of time when it's game day. It could be anytime, so you have to stay ready all the time. Your motivation needs to be continually high.

Question Number 4
  What do I think about explosive and impulsive acts when I'm angry?

Question Number 5
  When I get angry with people, how do I want to end up with them?

Question Number 6
  Where do I stand on sulking and pouting?

Question Number 7
  Am I willing to remain unaware of my anger sometimes?

Question Number 8
  Knowing how attached I am to behaviors which produce immediate gratification, what is my position with regard to short-term gains and long-term losses?

Question Number 9
  What is my position on hostility and hate?

Question Number 10
  Overall, what do I most want the outcome of my anger expression to be?

These strike me as ten important questions about anger. If you develop a clear-cut position on each of these, and if you get that position "planted" in your bones and muscles, you will inevitably become a "person in charge" of your anger expression.

This whole process involves three steps: (1) Develop your answer in response to each question; (2) Write a letter to yourself which carefully sets forth these answers; and (3) Commit yourself to reading this letter aloud to yourself once a week (perhaps every Monday morning) indefinitely. It is always good to have one other person hear you read your letter whenever possible.

My letter to myself appears in the next chapter. You can use it for ideas. But your letter may be entirely different from mine for many reasons. For instance, you may have learned to handle your anger by taking it out on your body, whereas I learned to explode or be underhanded. Or you may want to remain unaware of your anger sometimes, whereas I always want to be in touch with mine.

The point is to make your letter your own—one which accurately represents your beliefs and attitudes. It will have maximum effect that way. When we personally adopt new standards for self-evaluation, they will provide important self-regulative influence over our behavior. We will experience self-satisfaction from adhering to them and self-dissatisfaction from engaging in conduct opposed to them.

This process will work if you stay with it. You can gain control over your anger—literally turn your anger into an ally. When I went through this training, I found that an enormously attractive reward. I hope it is for you too.

A Letter to Myself

Dear Neil,

I am writing this letter to help you become an expert in handling your anger. I am proud of you for aspiring to this goal, and I am convinced that you are going to be successful in reaching it. Your life will be different as you learn to use your anger constructively.

What we both recognize is that you enjoy being angry sometimes. When you feel physiologically aroused, you are aware of suddenly having incredible power available. You're convinced that you can have an enormous impact with this kind of capacity at your command.

But it is crucial that you remain in control of how you express this anger: When it just comes firing out, you can do some stupid things. When your old habits take over, you become a slasher—using words to hurt and humiliate and punish. And you've been known to pound a desk and yell a little too.

But when you use your aroused state to help you move toward your goals, you can be a strong person. It all depends on how much in control you remain.

What you've learned is that unless you do plenty of work out in front of the time you're angry, you "go off" half-cocked.

You act foolishly. And then you feel disappointed in yourself. You vow never to do that again. But most of the time you don't do anything about it until the next "again." And that's too late.

So now you have agreed to exert all the energy necessary to stay out in front of the action. You know it will be demanding, but you also know how determined you are to get this anger business under control. In fact, it has become your personal growth frontier. You're convinced that if you can develop expertise in this area, you can get any part of your life under full control. So all the energy necessary, for as long as it takes, will be made available by you.

Here's what I understand you to be committed to—*no* more explosions or impulsive acts when you're angry. Your goal is to study all the techniques available for catching your anger and redirecting it at an early stage in the process. You do *not* wish to engage in any more "shoot from the hip" behavior.

Your strong desire is to be involved in constructive interaction with any person toward whom you experience anger. If they hurt you, you are determined to work it through with them so that it is less likely to happen next time. You would like to end up with their feeling more friendly to you at the end than at the beginning. You are convinced that if you can keep communicating with them, together you can work out a fair resolution of your problem which will leave both of you satisfied. Staying in the struggle is what you are committed to doing.

And you've decided that sulking and pouting are immature and unproductive behaviors which you won't engage in any more. They are designed to get attention and to try to pressure other people to do it your way. They're also designed to make life less enjoyable for others without your having to take responsibility for that result. You're through with all that. It doesn't work well for you or your relationships.

Furthermore, you *do not* wish to be unaware of any of your anger. Whatever is going on in you, you want to be in on it. If you don't know about it, you can't take advantage of it. And more than that, it will end up taking advantage of you. Your whole desire is to make anger a constructive experience—one designed to remove any problems in your path so that you can really enjoy life. Why would you ever want to remain unaware of anger. You wouldn't!

You are attached to immediate gratification. You like to be rewarded, and *right now*. That's your biggest enemy, and you need to stay continually on guard against it. When you were a kid, you learned to let fly with your anger because it brought immediate results. That it cost you a lot later didn't seem to change the way you expressed your anger. But now you want to opt for the long-term gains. If you miss a thrill or two in the moment, so what? Especially if you know that you'll be delighted a little later.

Hostility and hate are totally destructive. They hurt the person who holds them worse than they hurt anyone else. If they are caused by the buildup of "resentment residue" after inadequately handled anger episodes, you are all the more eager to process your anger so that no resentment is left over.

Overall, then, what you want is to experience anger when it is called for, stay in complete control of how you express it, eliminate explosive behavior, process that anger out to its edges, and end up in a better place than you started. You want to see yourself, and be seen by others, as a person who knows where he stands, who can allow others their freedom, and who seems determined to move decisively and deliberately against any problem spot which keeps him from living fully and loving freely.

Always remember this: No matter what others do, you can be an expert in handling your anger! You will become more and more effective as a person the longer you continue this effort.

I wish you genuine success.

Your friend,
Neil

ANGER MANAGEMENT PRINCIPLE NUMBER 3

Stay in Close Touch with Your Feelings

A critical aspect of anger-expression mastery is learning to sense when anger is approaching from within you. What you can't afford is any surprise attack. You need every second you can get to think through your strategy, because your challenge will be to make a series of critical decisions about how to handle enormous power so that the outcome will be highly positive. And you will need to make these decisions under great stress without any unnecessary delay.

The best way I know to detect anger in its earliest phases is to stay in close touch with your feelings all the time—especially when you are involved in transactions which might lead to trouble. When you learn to read your feelings in any given moment, you will automatically have available scores of details concerning you which will render decision making about constructive behavior sequences far more effective.

But how do you stay in close touch with your feelings? Let me tell you first about a structure which I think will help, and then I'll pass along five suggestions for maximizing the positive results you experience from the time you spend within this structure.

The two exercises I have in mind involve a pen and a journal. I will describe the first of these exercises in this chapter and detail the second one in the next chapter.

This exercise calls for you to spend time each day writing out your feelings just as you have them. So the first thing to do is to buy yourself a large notebook (or journal) just for this purpose. It should be used for the two exercises every day, and for nothing else.

You should find a place to keep your journal between times so that it remains totally private. If you fear that others might read it, explain to them what it is and ask for their pledge that they won't read it under any conditions.

The exercise requires an hour a day, at least six days a week, for a minimum of three months. That sounds like a tremendous amount of time, I know, but you are trying to take a huge step in the direction of knowing yourself—and sufficient time must be scheduled to do it well. If you have only a half hour a day, use that. It will give you an important start, and you may be able to expand your time later.

By the way, spend *exactly* the time you allot for this exercise. When time is up, put all materials away until the next day, even if you are right in the middle of a sentence.

Make sure that you are alone for these periods. Be as much to yourself as you possibly can be.

Now here are some suggestions about how to use these private times with your journal.

First, record the exact date and time above each day's entry.

Then make it your objective to record your feelings—whatever is going on for you at the time you're writing. And your challenge is to stay in touch with your *present* feelings. If that means you have to change subjects a lot, that's fine. You are writing this for no one but you.

Secondly, it is best to stay as relaxed as possible. But it is also essential to be alert. That's why writing in bed may not be such a good idea, while writing in the park near your home may be perfect.

Listen to your feelings while you write. Let your body talk. Follow your feelings out to their edges. Track them wherever they take you.

It doesn't matter whether your feelings are negative or positive, pleasant or unpleasant. You're simply trying to get to know them, whatever they are.

Now my experience in helping people with this exercise is that some persons tend to pick it up quite naturally, while others have a miserable time getting into it. The latter must be patient and persistent. The exercise virtually always works for everyone eventually. The secret is to stay at it.

Some individuals have difficulty, I think, because they have been taught to deny their feelings. Society tends to have a deep distrust of feelings. So the feelings of certain persons become buried and hard to reach.

It should be pointed out in response to this distrust that I never encourage anyone to let their feelings control their behavior. Quite to the contrary! But our goal here is to help you get in close touch with your affect, assuming that is the best way for you to "see" your anger coming.

In just a few pages I will tell you how to use your thinking to channel your anger constructively.

But right now I hope you are motivated to get yourself moving on this crucial three-month (at least) inner adventure. It will pay surprising dividends.

Keep an Anger Diary

The second exercise involving your journal operates on the principle that people who decide to work on the way they express their anger need a way to monitor their performance. I know of no better way than through the keeping of an anger diary—a daily accounting in your journal of actual anger experiences of that day.

When people come to me and request assistance in modifying their habitual way of expressing anger, I always encourage them to start immediately recording pertinent facts about every anger episode. And I ask them to commit themselves to keeping that account current for six months.

My reasons for suggesting this plan are straightforward and simple. There are basically three:

1. The detailed data give you an opportunity to review your performance in comparison to the training ideals. If something is going wrong, you want to know what it is.
2. When you become accustomed to jotting down your anger experiences, you will find that your expectation of recording a particular event will begin to influence the event itself. You simply cannot record your anger night

after night without changing your way of behaving the next day.

3. When you record your anger by using the brief format I'm going to suggest, you steep yourself in the "treatment plan." You go over and over the steps, and those steps become a part of you. Since these are the same steps you use in handling your anger in the moment you experience it, the repetition each night makes them easily available in the heat and stress of the "angry moment."

So how do you keep this anger account? Just follow these simple steps:

1. Use a section in your journal, or any other little notebook, which only you will ever see.

2. Keep it by your bedside, always immediately available.

3. Write in your anger diary at the same time every day. I have found the best time for most people to be when they go to bed each night. The experience which triggers their memory of the diary is climbing into bed. They *do not* get into bed without writing in their diary. Even if they experienced no anger that day, it is important to enter the date and "No anger today."

4. Follow a simple format:
    A. Date?
    B. When?
    C. With whom?
    D. What was my response?
    E. Why was I angry?
    F. What did I wish to accomplish with my anger?
    G. What strategy did I formulate?
    H. Did I implement my plan?

5. Here's an example:
    A. Tuesday, June 15th.
    B. 4:15 P.M.
    C. Lady on first floor.
    D. I was furious with her. I fumed and fussed for a while during the time I was thinking.

E. I was frustrated when she put the sign on the washer saying that no one can wash after 8 P.M.

F. I really just want enough time to get my clothes washed, without hassle, at a time convenient to me.

G. I decided to see the manager about getting Wednesdays since no one is signed up for that day, and I am free on Wednesdays. I will also check with local laundries to see how much it would cost to have some of my clothes washed there.

H. Not yet. I'll report in tomorrow night.

If you keep a brief account of each of your anger experiences, you will collect in one place a treasure house of information about yourself. This information will eventually give you substantial understanding of your way of handling anger.

Goal: Catch Anger at the First Sign

When you are able "to see anger coming"—to detect it at an early point—you have a significantly greater opportunity to use it constructively. Because of your foresight you can prepare to resist habitual ways of expressing it, especially if those ways have proven to be destructive. You also have time to strategize about the most effective ways of using your anger in the pursuit of personal and relational objectives.

So the most pressing questions become: How do I develop this ability to sense the approach of anger? And how do I identify the first sign of my anger?

In my experience the ability to sense a developing experience of anger is the result of: (1) Staying close to my feelings; (2) Isolating critical patterns by reflecting on numerous anger experiences from the past; and (3) Learning to place more and more confidence in my "discoveries."

You come to know what the first sign of anger is for you by carefully studying case after case of your anger. You perform a kind of anger autopsy. Eventually, you discover what the important first signs usually are for you. Fortunately, most people get angry in highly consistent ways from one time to the next—which makes the kind of analysis I'm talking about so beneficial.

For instance, one of my clients—a thirty-eight-year-old medical technician who was married and the mother of two teen-aged children—came to me suffering from a failing body and a failing marriage. It didn't take long, especially after I began to see her husband also, to discover that these two persons were locked in a complex interpersonal battle which seldom surfaced.

Jess, a middle-level executive, was agonizingly frustrated in his job—unable to please upper management, unhappy with specific job assignments, and underpaid. I found him to be a shy but stubborn man.

Louise was far more assertive, more successful at her job, more unhappy with the marriage, and suffering from stomach ulcers and colitis, the original reason her internist had referred her to me.

It became obvious over time that Louise was regularly angry with Jess but never dealt with that anger openly in her relationship with him. Instead of talking about her frustrations, she would deny to herself that she had any. But nevertheless, her body would become prepared to act. And her stomach and colon eventually began to break down. She desperately needed to alter that pattern.

Louise was highly motivated to change. Her suffering was intense.

We worked at first on helping her stay in close touch with her feelings so that she could better monitor her own internal process. Then we began to look for dynamic patterns as we inspected the daily records from her diary immediately before those days when she experienced especially pronounced physical pain.

What we discovered from the records was that less than a week prior to flare-ups of her physical symptoms there was a period of increasing frustration. And in nearly every case this frustration was related to a communications breakdown on Jess's part. He would become totally quiet for two or three days at a time and cut himself off entirely from Louise and the children. He would go to work, come home, watch television, and hurry to bed.

Louise would seethe, and her frustration would lead to general physiological arousal. Her whole organism was prepared to do something about the decaying relationship. But years before she had decided to "keep the peace" in relation to Jess, and that meant that she would never confront him. She became physically frozen in place, as it were—ready to act but resistant to the only actions on her part which made any sense. And her body bore the brunt of the unresolved dilemma which kept her in that state of readiness.

Once we had isolated this pattern, we were well on the way to solving the problem. Now the only two unanswered questions were: (1) Could we develop a strategy which would allow Louise to use her anger constructively—one that would help resolve the frustration she experienced when Jess went underground? and (2) If we could develop such a strategy, would her body relax so that her stomach and colon problems could subside?

The strategy we developed was complex, but it was basically this: When Louise sensed her frustration beginning to build, she told Jess about it and invited him to let her in on what was happening for him. She was encouraged to let Jess manage his own career problem and to communicate only her general support of him and her desire to be in close communication with him as he worked through his problem.

Jess began to communicate, and as he did, his own sense of feeling emotionally frozen and unable to move became clear. When he recognized that he had a substantial career problem, he asked for my advice about how to proceed. I encouraged him to find specialized career counseling to help resolve his long-term employment dilemma.

The momentum began to swing in a positive direction when for fifteen successive days Louise had no negative physical symptoms. This was a three-year record for her. Jess was still frustrated in his job, but he was more hopeful because of an

M.A. program he had started as a result of his career counseling.

But most important was the fact that Louise now felt free to confront Jess when he became silent. And she was gaining confidence in her ability to catch her anger at an early point, direct it in a constructive way, and break the old routine of preparing her body for action without ever acting. She was establishing new records for remaining symptom-free because she was expressing her anger effectively.

This brief case description will perhaps give you some sense of how anger can be detected in its early phases through a careful search for patterns, and how a program can be developed for reversing destructive expressions which have become habituated through repeated use.

I could share with you numerous examples of persons who demonstrated that damaging ways of expressing anger can be altered. And what I have found common to all successful efforts is early intervention in the anger sequence before it has a chance to develop that "rapid-fire" quality which makes it feel so automatic and unstoppable.

ANGER MANAGEMENT PRINCIPLE NUMBER 4

Put Your Massive Brain in Gear

You have a massive brain capable of tremendous feats. If you are like most persons, you regularly use but a fraction of your brain's potential power.

With your brain you can become aware of your feelings, and you can learn to think in ways that will put *you* in charge of how you express those feelings. Through the disciplined use of your rational powers you can develop the ability to use your arousal state (which we have labeled as "anger") to resolve the problems which confront you and cause you to experience hurt, frustration, and fear.

When it comes to anger expression, the challenge you face is to learn to use your rational capacity effectively in dealing with the following two major areas:

1. First, you must dissolve highly patterned behavioral sequences. These sequences have undoubtedly proven to be unproductive, even destructive, but they have such a hold on you that you have had a hard time giving them up.

   That's because they have been carefully learned—undoubtedly when you were very young. They were learned because someone modeled them for you, you tried them, and you experienced some momentary positive results from them. This immediate gratification established an expectation in your mnid. Now, even though you know that the long-term effects of these behavioral sequences will be negative, you are still hooked on your own expectation of the short-term gratification you expect to receive. These destructive habitual ways of expressing your anger must be reversed. And that will require a concentrated use of your rational capacity.

2. New and more constructive behavioral sequences must be substituted for these former ways of expressing your anger. And these new patterns must be learned so well that they come to seem as automatic as the former ones.

This kind of learning still takes place in the most effective way when you are available to demonstrate the new behaviors, and reinforcements for your behavior come from the situation in which you find yourself. Unfortunately, there aren't many models available to demonstrate constructive anger approaches. And the reinforcement you receive for these new behaviors will often come only over the long term.

This means that you must learn to serve your own needs in both of these ways—as a model for yourself and as a reinforcing agent for your own behavior.

And that is where your rational powers become so important. You *can* supply both of these needs through the use of your rational capacity, but it will require a high-level effort.

Most people I encounter have spent little time developing their high-level rational powers. They have not been encouraged to take control of their lives this way.

And that's why their feelings often get expressed in whatever way they learned to express them when they were young. If they learned to explode, somatize, punish themselves, or express their anger in an underhanded way, they still do. They have never been encouraged to use their rational power to intervene in the old behavioral sequences and take control of the way they express their anger.

So I want you to put your massive brain in gear. When you are engaged in a provocative dialogue and you experience that first sign of anger, it is essential to maintain a task orientation. You have a big job to do.

These next chapters are designed to help you engage in a conditioning program which will make your thinking center strong and alert.

The first thing you can do is to begin thinking about being in control of how you express your feelings. You can start sensing that with the power you have you are going to intervene in and dissolve the old habits, and you are going to initiate new patterns which will contribute significantly to the effectiveness of your coping in the world.

The fact is that when you begin thinking about thinking, you *have* put your mind in gear. And that is an essential step in taking full control of expressing your anger.

If It Reads "Red-hot Anger," Delay Any Response

If you've had time to finish the exercises designed to improve your self-concept, I hope you agree that the "self" area is basic. And I hope you've finished working out your set of anger "intentions" and written to yourself about them. If you've also started writing in a journal each day and keeping an anger diary you are *really* on the move! That just leaves "putting your mind in gear" and "learning to catch your anger at the first sign."

However many of these suggestions you've found time to implement, pat yourself on the back. It means you're committed to your own growth, and that's a very positive sign.

If you haven't implemented some parts of the program yet, I hope you will be able to take advantage of them as soon as possible. My strong encouragement to you grows out of my deep conviction that each of these exercises will put one more part of the puzzle together for you. When you've fully solved that puzzle, you will experience a deep sense of accomplishment which will itself generate within you a strong feeling of joy.

This next step in the process seems simple, but it isn't so

simple when the pressure is on and the old habits are straining for expression.

It is this: When you pick up a feeling from inside yourself that tells you anger is coming, *delay any behavioral response.*

What you're looking for at that point is *time.* Your objective is to defeat those habituated responses of yours—totally derail them. You need time to do that.

And you want to direct your anger in a way that will handle your dilemma effectively. It takes time to come up with the right strategy.

So when you see anger coming, the first thing you want to do is buy time.

This is an age-old remedy for getting a better grip on a situation when you're angry. Old-timers advised that you "count to ten" or "bite your lip." There are some other ideas about how to delay which I will mention in the next chapter. But the essential point is that you *consciously refuse to do what you used to do which didn't work.* If you used to explode, don't. If you used to prepare for action and then didn't act, leaving your body in a constant state of alert, don't. If you used to call yourself names and demand ever more of yourself, don't. If you used to express your anger in sneaky, underhanded ways, don't.

When you're staying close to your feelings and your inner gauge registers "Red-hot Anger Ahead," delay any behavioral response. You are in control—and you want a little time to calculate. Your new ways of expressing anger aren't automatic yet. And your old ways are. You stand at a critical junction. And with sufficient time available, you will transform your anger and allow it to serve your loftiest goals.

Select a Key Word to Trigger an Alternate Program

Roger Jessor, a thirty-five-year-old pilot for a major airline, called me for an appointment after he heard me speak on anger at a Rotary Club meeting.

"I know when I'm becoming angry," Roger said. "I can sense it building a long time ahead on most occasions. But I can't seem to do anything about it. I am so programmed to explode that I feel like a runaway train is coming through my station. It's going a hundred miles an hour, and it is impervious to any signals."

Roger was telling a story I had heard before. The old anger-expression habits build up so much steam over the years that the idea of slowing them down seems hopeless. But I'm convinced that everyone can do it. It takes regular practice and rigid discipline.

"Here's what I want you to think of doing," I told Roger. "When you see that train coming—while it's still a mile down the tracks—you pull a lever to shift it to a sidetrack. And then slow it down until it eventually stops. When it does, start making preparations to get another train moving."

I shared with Roger my experience of needing to find a key word which was equivalent to pulling that "sidetrack lever."

There are thousands of possibilities, but the word I've fastened on for myself is "think." When I see the runaway anger train coming, I immediately say to myself, *"Think!"*

The first thing I think to do is stop the old behavior sequence—in Roger's case, exploding. I simply won't let that behavior run over me the way it wants to.

Then I move through a carefully rehearsed sequence which I'm going to present in the next few chapters.

"Do you think that would work for me?" Roger asked.

"Of course," I told him, and I invited him to practice a little.

He told me about three or four anger episodes from the last month or so of his life—times when he had exploded. One involved his estranged wife when she refused to let him take his little girl in connection with his regular weekend visiting rights. Another outburst was directed at his copilot, who was uncooperative during a whole trip and persisted in wisecracking with the stewardesses. And a third involved another motorist who was "driving too fast and endangering my life."

In every one of these cases Roger had totally relinquished control, and his behavior had caused him great embarrassment. In one case that behavior had resulted in a significant amount of legal trouble.

We backtracked in each example to the earliest point at which Roger had sensed his anger starting to build. He rehearsed actually saying outloud "Think!" at that point.

What "think" meant to him was "sidetrack that runaway train. And then get ready to put another train on the track to deliver my anger in an effective and constructive way."

Think! A key word for emergency situations—designed to trigger an alternate program with a far greater likelihood of producing positive results.

On Developing
a Constructive Alternative

When the runaway anger expression was still a mile down the tracks, you pulled the lever which sidetracked it. And you slowed it to a stop.

But that doesn't mean you dissolved your anger. You did make sure that your destructive way of expressing anger was controlled, and by doing that, you accomplished something vitally important.

But presumably, whatever it was that contributed to your anger still exists. And your anger still exists. So now your challenge is to develop a way of expressing that anger so that the source of your hurt, frustration, or fear can be taken care of fully.

This is where the great payoff for all your hard work will be realized. It is right here that anger can be transformed into a constructive force and used to resolve the problem which exists. This is the critical point. Take your time.

You are in control—remember that. By *thinking* carefully throughout these moments, you will be able to develop a way of expressing your anger which will accomplish what anger is meant to accomplish.

If at any point in this process you sense you are losing control, remind yourself to do one thing—*think*.

My own experience has led me to devise a three-step thought process. (Each of these is spelled out in one of the next chapters.)

1. *Why* am I angry? Focus on hurt, frustration, and fear.
2. *What* do I want from this encounter?
3. *How* can I get what I want? That is, What is an effective strategy?

There is nothing easy about developing an alternative way to express anger. But this is where your expertise will be demonstrated. And everything that we worked on earlier was simply getting you ready for this moment.

Why Am I Angry? Focus on Hurt, Frustration, and Fear

I can imagine what you're saying as you sit there reading this: "In the middle of my being fighting angry, he expects me to *think!* More than that, he wants me to think about *why* I'm angry. I'm ready to yell at somebody, just land all over them, and I'm supposed to 'focus on my hurt, frustration, and fear.'"

As hard as that sounds, you can do it. Even if it seems virtually impossible to you right now, it can be exactly what you do when you get angry even later today.

Remember, when you experience anger, your first job is to stop the runaway train—your habituated, destructive response. That will buy you some time.

Then your second job is to formulate an alternate way of expressing your anger—one which is designed to manage the problem in relation to which you are now angry.

The more clearly you can think during this part of the process, the more likely you are to come up with an effective way to handle the situation. If your experience is like mine, your thinking will sometimes be crystal clear under the stress of these conditions, but at other times it will be foggy. The secret will be to stay as relaxed as possible. Your best thinking will take place when your anxiety level is lowest—or at least within the optimal range.

No question is more basic than this one to your thinking: Why am I angry?

There are millions of possible reasons, all or only one of which may have contributed to your anger. It would be an impossible task to ferret out the specific reasons unless you can begin with a significantly narrowed search area.

And you can. Nine times out of ten you will be angry because you have been hurt, frustrated, or threatened.

Beginning with this assumption, you can expect to find the crucial contributing factors in one of these three areas. If I'm angry, I always ask myself: What am I feeling hurt, frustrated, or fearful about? When I experience any of the three of these feelings, I "almost automatically" become angry—and I do that so I will be ready to respond to whatever is contributing to my feeling that way. My objective is to get beyond these unpleasant feelings.

Now, when you find out why you have become angry, you are ready for the next question. And the answer to this "why" question will carefully focus your thinking about the "what" question which comes next.

Here are two brief illustrations:

1. Martha, thirty-two and married, baked two pies and decided to take one to her mother, who lived alone. She had been there only a few minutes, but her mother had not turned off the TV, and she had told Martha how tired she looked.

Martha could feel herself starting to get angry. She sidetracked her habituated response, which was suddenly to tell her mother she had to go, and then to leave. This would have meant an afternoon of seething for Martha and the likelihood of a headache.

Having sidetracked that response, Martha began to think. She asked herself why she was angry—what she was hurt, frustrated, or fearful about. In a flash she discovered three contributing factors. She wanted to communicate with her mother, but she was frustrated with the "blaring" of the TV. She was proud of her pies and her thoughtfulness, and she wanted her mother to notice, be pleased, and compliment her on both. She was hurt when she didn't. Finally, it hurt her that her mother criticized how she looked by pointing out how tired she appeared.

With this information available Martha was ready for the second question, which we will consider in the next chapter.

2. Bill, a twenty-two-year-old who had just graduated from college and moved back to his hometown, was at lunch with Jack, a friend, when Jack happened to mention that Sally, a girl Bill had dated during the past two summers and several shorter vacations, had also been dating another friend of Bill's. When he heard this, Bill could no longer concentrate on eating or on talking with Jack. And the longer he sat there, the more he experienced himself becoming angry.

Over the next few hours, Bill managed to block two responses which would have been natural for him. One was to try forgetting about Sally, never to call her again, and simply start dating someone else. The other response was in addition to the first—to call the friend who had been dating Sally and let him have it for his "disloyalty."

Bill asked himself why he was angry—what he was hurt, frustrated, or fearful about. He located four items. One, he felt threatened that Sally might be more interested in the other guy, and afraid that he had lost her. Two, he was hurt that she had dated someone else when, although they had no formal agreement, he thought they both viewed their relationship as "special." Three, he was frustrated with these complications because he had looked forward eagerly to getting home and taking Sally out again. Four, he was hurt that his friend, whom he was sure knew that he had been dating Sally, had selfishly "moved in."

Now Bill too was prepared to move to the second question.

In these examples, Martha and Bill had successfully blocked their habitual anger responses, and they had each asked the fundamental question—"Why am I angry?" Assuming they are able to manage equally well the next two phases in the process of selecting a constructive alternative, the outcome of their efforts should be decidedly positive.

What Do I Want
from This Encounter?

Let's assume you know *why* you're angry. That gives you highly valuable information about your situation.

Armed with that information, you are ready to confront the second critical question: "*What* do I want from this encounter?"

Right now this question has become the most important one you could ask. That's because you are ready for it. The timing is right. If this question gets asked too early, before you have answered the "why" question, it can lead to inaccurate answers and negative consequences.

It is right here—as you think about this question—that your set of anger values will prove especially helpful to you. From a values standpoint the most helpful way to ask this question is: "What do I want from this encounter which will contribute most to the kind of long-term relationship I want to have with this person?"

There are so many potential answers. Let me mention a few which often press for implementation—inner urges we feel so tempted to act on—but almost always prove destructive:

1. I want to hurt him just as badly as I can.
2. I want to show her what a rotten person she is.

3. I want to make him feel guilty about what he has done.
4. I want to pretend that I have no anger at all even though I do.
5. I am so angry that I'm not going to do one thing she wants me to.
6. I'm angry, and I just want to stay angry for a good long time.
7. I want to humiliate her—make her pay for what she did to me.

But there are other answers to this "what" question which are less immediately available when we're angry but almost always lead to constructive results.

1. I am so hurt. I want to use my anger so that I don't have to be hurt any longer.
2. I want to leave this encounter with my frustration worked through.
3. I want to make it through this anger episode without any guilt.
4. What she did really scared me. I want to use my anger in a way that will reduce my chances of having to be frightened next time.
5. I want to show them that they're wrong, that what I'm saying is legitimate.
6. I want to help her change her behavior so that I don't have to be hurt by her.
7. I want to get this problem out of the way so that I can get about the task of loving her again.

Consider the two persons I mentioned in the last section.

1. Once Martha had figured out why she was angry in relation to her mother, she could figure out *what* she wanted to use her anger for. "I want to be able to talk with mother freely and easily without the television interrupting," Martha could say to herself. "And I want to learn to think about her needs and learn to give to her without needing her to recognize 'how good I am' and

make over me. I don't want to be so dependent on her. For instance, I want to take a look at myself when I get home to see if I look tired. If I do, I want to take better care of myself. If I don't, there's no need to let mother's comment have any effect on me."

2. When Bill had become clear about why he was angry, he could also focus on the "what" question. "What I want is clear information," he might have said. "I don't want to act on the basis of rumors. And I don't want to end up losing any friendships either. But I do want to work hard to get what I want. I want Sally if I can reasonably have her. I want to understand why she dated my friend. I want to clear the air with him—let him know I feel betrayed by him but still end up with his friendship. I want to get all of this taken care of as soon as possible. And I want to get it done with class—in a way that leaves me feeling good about myself and with no guilt."

Now these two know what they want to use their anger to accomplish. They are ready to formulate a strategy for implementing their answers. And the question about strategy is the one we will consider in the next chapter.

How Can I Get What I Want?

Now you know *why* you're angry and *what* you want from your anger. You're ready for the "how" question. "How can I use my anger to get as much of what I want from it as possible?" What you need is a strategy to guide you in using your anger constructively.

I'm assuming that the list of what you want revolves around your long-term best interests. If it does, you will feel like, and *be*, a winner every time you check off one of the items on your "want list." And this process will serve to provide immediate feedback along the way about how your strategy is working.

There are countless strategies for every experience of anger. You can certainly explode, or you can pretend you have no anger—and there are several subcategories of each of these. Then you can talk out your feelings with the other person or write them out on your own. Strategies are available by the score.

Let me describe an experience which calls for the development of an anger-expression strategy.

Imagine that your seventeen-year-old son is out on one of his first dates. He has the family car. You told him that you wanted him home by twelve midnight at the latest. He agreed.

You're unable to go to sleep when you get to bed at ten forty-five. The fact that he hasn't driven much by himself keeps your anxiety too high for you to relax. As soon as midnight comes and he gets home, you will be relieved. Then you'll get right to sleep.

But midnight comes and goes with no sound of Ron or the car. At twelve-ten you think to yourself that you want to teach him to be prompt—not to agree to a set time and then arrive ten minutes after that time.

At twelve-thirty the promptness issue has been forgotten, and your anger is beginning to build. You just can't believe that Ron would be so insensitive to your feelings and to the agreement you made with him.

At one o'clock your anger is replaced by anxiety. You are deeply concerned about his safety—and the safety of his date. You decide that if he isn't home by one-fifteen, you will call her family to see if Ron and their daughter had arrived there safely. You are really worried.

At one-fourteen, with your left hand on the telephone, you hear the car in the driveway. Your first sense is great relief. His safety is an answer to prayer. But your relief sigh is not totally spent when it turns to anger—red-hot anger. Now *you* are your problem.

Here comes your runaway train! What you feel like doing is exploding all over that seventeen-year-old son you were so worried about two minutes ago.

Ron is carefully putting the car in the garage. Between now and the time he gets to the house, you have four big issues to *think* about. First, you will need to deal with your habitual explosiveness. The challenge will be to sidetrack that response. What you know is that explosions have little positive impact, almost always alienate, and turn out to be essentially foolish.

Then you will need to ask yourself *why* you are angry. You've worked on that for the last hour and fifteen minutes.

You are hurt that Ron has been so insensitive to your feelings. You are frustrated that a perfectly good agreement broke down so completely. And you have been, until two minutes ago, terribly afraid that something was seriously wrong.

Thirdly, you will move to *what* you want from the expression of your anger. Let's assume you want three matters fully resolved: (1) You want to know that Ron understands and appreciates the depth and strength of your feelings about time limits; (2) You want to make sure that all agreements you make with him from now on are carefully kept; and (3) You want to emphasize the fact that his lateness threatens you and makes you fearful about his safety—and you would like not to experience that kind of anxiety again.

Fourthly, you will think about *how* you can best accomplish these three goals. Here are some ways *not* to do it:

1. Put Ron down, humiliate him, and "work at him." This will undoubtedly escalate the problem.
2. Punish him. This seldom leads to consequences which are as positive as those produced by rewards.
3. Try to carry on a meaningful discussion at one-thirty in the morning. This usually leads to little more than a lecture and maybe a few harsh, mumbled words in response.
4. Let the matter go until another time and then never take it up. This won't work either.

And here are some ideas designed to get the job done effectively:

1. Greet Ron with two comments: (1) "I'm relieved to see you, because I was worried about you"; and (2) "I am very upset by your lateness, and I want to talk to you about it tomorrow morning at ten." If he agrees, fine; if he offers another time, try to adjust to that time. The important thing is to make sure you end up with a set time the next day.
2. Prepare well for that meeting.

3. When you meet with him, let him know at the outset that the meeting can be brief—or last longer if he would like. Ron will need some sense of control.

4. Let him know what your three-point agenda is (from your list of wants).

5. Establish the fact that driving the car is a reward to be given for good behavior. And you want to be able to give him that reward whenever he keeps his end of your agreements with him.

6. Establish with him your expectation that he will be completely responsible about time limits and about agreements in general.

7. Listen carefully when he wishes to talk. Make sure you fully understand what he tries to say.

8. Treat him with dignity.

9. Be willing to take full responsibility for your own parental role.

My sense is that this strategy will offer ample opportunity for a full presentation of your thoughts and feelings, a full airing of Ron's responses, and a clarification of the important issues.

This is an example of *how* to strategize in connection with *what* you wish to accomplish with your anger.

Martha and Bill——Strategies for Getting What They Want

When Martha and Bill develop strategies for using their aroused state to get what they want, it will be crucial for them to take into consideration several variables:

1. The personalities of the important people involved.
2. Their particular relationship with these people.
3. The amount of time available.
4. The constraints of the situation.
5. How strongly invested they are in whether this turns out well.

Take Martha, for instance. She wants to communicate with her mother in an uninterrupted way. What she knows is that her mother is easily hurt by criticism. Martha is her only child, and Martha's father died only eighteen months ago. Martha has plenty of time this morning. Moreover, she knows that this will be just one of scores of times she will have like this with her mother. Obviously, she is heavily invested in its going well—maybe too heavily invested.

With these variables in mind, Martha decides that she will begin the conversation with her mother and then move to the living room and adjust the television. She first engages her mother: "Mom, how did you get along at the new bridge group yesterday?" And when her mother begins to answer, Martha unobtrusively turns the television down so that her mother can have the sense of being heard more easily. Both of them are relieved to be able to talk without interference.

Martha's strategy for dealing with her own overdependence on her mother is a more complex one. What Martha knows instinctively is that her hurt about not being appreciated, and her additional hurt in connection with her mother's comment about her "looking tired," are essentially and ultimately her own problems. These can be handled at home under less pressure.

The next day Martha begins to develop a strategy for dealing with them. She decides to attack them in three ways: first, to reflect on them at length in her journal; second, to spend some time talking about them with her closest friend, a person she deeply trusts, who seems to have dealt well with her own mother; and third, to get some quiet time with her husband so that she can talk with him about these issues.

Our second illustration involves Bill. Clear about what he wishes to use his anger to accomplish, Bill first considers several important variables. For instance, he knows Sally is a seasoned group therapy member, and he doesn't have to be cautious around her. In fact, Sally appreciates getting everything "right out front." Bill knows too that Sally will give plenty of time to process the matter. And he is heavily invested in working it through with her. He is not as sure about the openness of his friend to this kind of processing, but their relationship is of long standing, and Bill feels comfortable in bringing the matter up.

Bill decides to arrange a date with Sally as soon as possible. He plans to ask her out for dinner and to tell her ahead of time that he has some things to talk over with her which may take the rest of the evening. He knows a great restaurant just outside of town where he can take her—where it is quiet but not too quiet—and where they can spend the evening eating and talking.

He plans to focus on the issues he has identified on his want list. He does not intend with Sally or his friend to "make them wrong" but to present his own feelings as clearly and nonthreateningly as possible, listen carefully to their responses, and search for resolution.

Bill has a strategy he feels good about.

Strategies are absolutely necessary in developing alternative ways of expressing anger, especially when these forms of anger expression are new and every step is like a first one—full of excitement and adventure.

When strategies have been formulated, they must be implemented—and that is our subject in the next chapter.

Press the Start Button

When you develop an anger-expression strategy which is solidly based on a careful, internal processing of your anger's "whys" and "whats," that strategy is invariably of great value. And it is crucial that your strategy be implemented.

But sometimes that implementation process involves anxiety-provoking experiences, and the temptation not to implement the strategy becomes a strong and pressing one. Strategies can demand so much of you—for instance, talking to Sally and your friend about an extremely sensitive and personal matter, or going to your boss with issues demanding a great deal from both of you.

And sometimes, as in the case of Ron coming home late, a parent, or anyone in equivalent circumstances, can reason that the confrontation the next day really isn't necessary. Ron won't be late again. And besides, the encounter will make waves for the entire family.

That's dangerous thinking! If you give in to it, you will inevitably let yourself down. Not to carry out your strategy will leave you with unresolved hurt, frustration, and fear. It will also increase the chances that your anger experience will return—and next time it will be much more difficult to handle.

For anger which gets analyzed in the head but never gets

implemented behaviorally not only is kept from doing the work for which it was intended, but it will often be expressed destructively in ways less controlled by conscious choice.

That's what happened to Martha. After sidetracking her destructive anger response—the "quick exit"—she processed the "why," "what," and "how" questions precisely and effectively. Then she successfully implemented that aspect of her strategy which directly involved her mother.

The other aspect of her strategy, involving the internal handling of her own overdependence on her mother, never got implemented. Martha had carefully outlined the ways in which she planned to proceed—talks with self, friend, and husband—but she just never "got around to it." And today Martha's dependency dilemma remains as unresolved as ever, actually handicapping her in a number of significant relationships. Thus, her unexpressed anger, never having done the work it could have done, leaves her dependency needs "untreated"—and this overdependency regularly sabotages her most important relationships.

But Bill's story is a far more successful one. He opened up completely with Sally, discovered that her feelings for him were far stronger than the feelings she had for his friend, and thus succeeded in using his anger state to develop a relationship with Sally characterized by deeper understanding and greater commitment.

Bill felt as satisfied with the way he handled his anger toward his friend, but the results were not as positive. While there is no remaining animosity between them, they have never enjoyed the same degree of friendship as before. But Bill is pleased about the way the two of them related over this very difficult matter—and neither of them feels any guilt or unresolved anger.

The essential message in all of this is: When you formulate a strategy for expressing your anger which is designed to help you get what you want, be sure to press the start button. For anger-expression strategies which are the result of clear and careful thinking will inevitably lead to growth and progress. They deserve to be implemented.

ANGER MANAGEMENT PRINCIPLE NUMBER 5

Learn How to Forgive the Bum

You can learn to express your anger constructively. And that can make an incredible difference in your life.

Even after you have mastered anger expression, one remaining challenge will require your best effort—learning how to forgive. Forgiveness is crucial.

Here's why. Your physiological arousal which we have labeled "anger" will dissipate with effective expression. And you will be free of anger. That is exactly what we want for you, of course—and the sooner the better in every case!

But that same physiological state can be regenerated on later occasions if you ruminate over the incident which contributed to your anger. If you remember in detail the insulting treatment which hurt you, you can work yourself into a rage all over again.

And you will inevitably do this if you have not let the experience go. I know of no better way to let it go than to forgive the person who insulted you. When you do, you benefit substantially, because you don't have to be angry any longer in response to this hurtful event. Of course, the other person benefits too, because your relationship with her will inevitably improve.

Forgiveness offers many benefits:

1. It sets you free from the past—from hurt, frustration, and fear—and from miserable experiences of many kinds.
2. It significantly reduces the total amount of anger you will experience in your life, because no painful event is allowed to contribute to your anger more than once.
3. It allows your mind—conscious and unconscious—to focus on the present, and that leads to more effective and rewarding living.
4. It sets your relationship with another person free to grow and develop.

But for many of us forgiveness is difficult. Somehow it seems unnatural. No one ever taught us how to forgive. And much of the time we really don't want to forgive the other person anyway. We want to hang on to our sense of having been wronged.

So we turn one stressful insult into a series of anger experiences. By our unwillingness and inability to forgive, we multiply our hurt and our pain, and preclude our freedom and all that freedom can offer.

Forgiveness can be learned. You have the ability to forgive. What is required is this:

1. A deep sense of *inner security* which allows you to set yourself and someone else free without your feeling less sure of yourself.
2. Sufficient inner *thinking* which carefully develops the "case for forgiving another" complete with a full recognition of the contributions forgiveness can make to your own sense of happiness.
3. A strong *will* informed by insight—an unyielding determination to engage in every process necessary to bring about total forgiveness.
4. The ability to empathize with another. I will offer some suggestions in this regard in the next section.

One last matter: Why "bum" in the title? Because that's the way we usually feel about a person we need to forgive. And when we have forgiven him, we may still call him a bum, but the word will have a totally different ring to it—a ring with overtones of understanding and affection. Such is the delight of forgiving.

Develop Empathy Skills—
"What Is He Feeling Now?"

The idea is as old as the hills: "To understand all is to forgive all."

When you understand why other people behave obnoxiously, you will inevitably find yourself experiencing less anger toward them. And your ability to forgive will be substantially improved. Moreover, your capacity to vicariously experience the other person's pain will place an important curb on any tendency you may have to express your anger aggressively in reaction. When we perceive that the other person is a lot like us, our empathy for them is greater, and it becomes very difficult for us to injure them in any way.

Additionally, several psychological studies have demonstrated that with cognitive clarification of the situation which contributed to your anger—that is, seeing it in a new way, perhaps from the other person's point of view—your *physiological state* dissipates significantly.

Charles and Wanda Taylor sought my help for a marriage that had become frozen after a series of hurtful encounters which had never been forgiven. I still remember my first session with them. They were stiff and formal with each other, almost unable to look each other in the eye and carry on a conversation. When they did talk during that hour, which wasn't often, they both looked at me. Their words were bullet-like, and you could almost see steam coming from their mouths—so cold were their feelings and thoughts. Their marriage was about to die, and they were in terrible pain as individuals too.

It became clear over the weeks that the Taylors were continually angry with one another. They could each cite dozens of ways the other person had failed to understand, failed to love, failed to "be there," failed to care. They were so busy nurturing their grudges against each other that they were unaware of how they were torturing themselves with their hate.

I set out to thaw the relational ice. I used every resource I had available. Because they were active Christians, I periodically quoted biblical passages like Jesus' encouragement to forgive another: "Even if he wrongs you seven times a day and each time turns again and asks forgiveness, forgive him." (Luke 17:4; The Living Bible.) And the Apostle Paul's famous instruction: "Be gentle and ready to forgive; never hold grudges. Remember, the Lord forgave you, so you must forgive others." (Colossians 3:13; The Living Bible.)

And in time, the ice did begin to thaw. As I listened to each of them and worked to understand what they were saying from their perspective, they felt less constrained to nurture their bitterness. And they profited from my modeling; they began to listen and to try to understand each other.

And each time they were able to understand a little, I sensed they forgave a little. And as they forgave, they felt released to love. And their growing love began to build a momentum of its own.

Understanding begets forgiving, and forgiving begets loving, and loving brings us close to one another—and "close to one another" is what healthy marriage is all about.

Charles and Wanda Taylor are happily married today—not without problems, but well equipped to work their problems through by honest conversation and genuine efforts to understand.

But how do you develop the ability to empathize with others, the skill to see an event from their point of view? If understanding what that person is feeling and thinking is so central to forgiveness, how do you learn to do it?

I have concluded from my experience that there are two prerequisites to learning empathy skills and four helpful training exercises in which you may wish to engage.

The two prerequisites are these:

1. You must genuinely want to understand the other person.
2. You must be patient—willing to allow persons to reveal themselves gradually, and in their own time.

The four exercises which can increase your ability to empathize are:

1. Working within yourself, well in advance of experiencing any anger, on the wisdom of understanding another person. You will undoubtedly consider the advantages of knowing what someone else is feeling and thinking while you are in the middle of an anger-provoking experience with them. It is important to become clear in your own mind about the place of empathy in the forgiveness process, and the importance of forgiveness in becoming the person you want to be.
2. Working on developing an attitude of "I want to understand what you are feeling" in relation to that person who is contributing to your anger.
3. Asking persons what they are feeling *while* you are angry with them, and making every effort to understand their feelings even though you are experiencing anger toward them.
4. Trying to summarize what you hear them saying, and asking them for feedback about the accuracy of your summaries—and clarification of those parts that you missed of what they were trying to communicate.

Forgiveness can do wonders for *you*. It can set you free to live in the present, and that's where abundant life is experienced most fully.

Mutual empathy and *mutual forgiveness* is the ultimate ideal. When you are able to help your "opponents" understand your side, they will also be able to forgive you. As you share your feelings fully, including your interpretation of the current situation, you will facilitate their understanding, forgiving process.

No path to forgiveness is straighter or truer than understanding. To learn how to be empathic, and then to practice that skill, can alter your way of relating to others significantly. It is a quality well worth the effort which is required to develop it.

A Sense of Mastery

When you gain mastery in your life, you are on the verge of joy—especially when that mastery involves a central aspect of your inner experience. Learning to manage your anger means that you get to sit in the driver's seat and take control of your life.

More than that, anger mastery tends to generalize. When you learn to use anger to clear your life of problems, you begin to recognize within you the potential for mastery of all your most pressing emotions.

This training program, which was designed to make you the master of your anger, is complete now. If you implement this program in your life, I am convinced that you will experience significant progress toward mastery. I know the program works.

But I can imagine that if anger has been a problem for you over a number of years, you may have read this book with a certain amount of skepticism. Perhaps you wondered if any of this can help *you*, given your unique difficulties.

Here's what I'd like to suggest. Set up a program for yourself such as I've described. Get started right now. Give it one month. If it's obviously working, add a month at a time. If your destructive anger patterns run deep, expect to stay at the task for considerably longer before you sense yourself to be a master—six months at a minimum.

One thing more. You have been introduced to these suggestions in an order I believe to be important. One exercise builds on another. If you start with the self-esteem exercises and move to the values-clarification section, then to the journal work, etc., the program will offer the greatest benefits.

So you now know how to transform your anger into a significant resource for constructive living. And you may already be experiencing some sense of mastery as you build this program into your own life. If you are, and especially if anger has been a miserable problem for you in the past, you know what a relief and thrill that mastery carries with it.

But If Anger Still Has a Hold on You and You Can't Break Free, Get Some Good Therapy Help

Some destructive anger-expression patterns are more difficult to extinguish than others. If, for instance, you learned when you were young to deny any awareness of your anger but your body often remained in an aroused state for hours with little relief, you may have developed a habit of doing that. And it will be difficult to overcome.

What probably happens is that when you deny your anger—and consequently the anger remains unexpressed—your denial behavior gets reinforced by the sense of relief you experience in not having to express the anger and be responsible for the consequences. Then, at a low level of awareness, you develop an expectation of relief whenever you engage in this denial pattern.

But the problem is that without your being aware of it, your body always gets activated. And because the source of that activation—the hurt, frustration, or fear—is never resolved by the expression of your anger, the physiologically aroused state continues. It is as though your body is alert for action, but your mind has long since denied any need to act.

So you're a tough person to deal with—even for you. It's hard to convince you that you even have any anger. It takes a case of ulcers, an internist's referral to a psychologist or psychiatrist, and an eventual diagnosis of "self-directed aggression." Even then you say to yourself, "Me? Angry? I've never been angry!" But because you were told by someone you trust that your anger is responsible for your physical condition, you picked up this book, read it, tried the program, but you're still feeling the physical discomfort. Your anger problem is resisting your best effort to rid yourself of it.

There are other anger problems which are very difficult to overcome. If you have one of these unusually "hard to crack" problems, let me encourage you to seek some good psychotherapeutic help.

Moreover, if you find yourself unable to get started on the program outlined on these pages, you may need another person to help motivate you. Of if you find yourself expressing your anger in some unusually destructive ways—hurting yourself or hurting others—you may need help immediately.

What kind of help do you need? What kind of helper should you look for?

My opinion is that most people need help implementing exactly what I've talked about in this book. You need someone right there with you—making keen observations, pointing out simple errors, offering encouragement, helping to keep you motivated.

The kind of psychotherapist I would recommend for you would be:

1. A solidly trained professional.
2. Someone with the basic human qualities of compassion and sensitivity.
3. Someone who is experienced in working with people who suffer from problems connected with the way they express their anger.
4. Someone who can offer an action program like the one presented in this book.

Let me encourage you to view the seeking of professional assistance for an anger problem, or any emotional problem, as a matter totally without stigma. If you have an unusually resistant pattern, it's highly likely that you learned it when you were very young and it was methodically reinforced. Many people require the help of a professional in overcoming that kind of early learning.

The crucial point is to be persistent in ridding yourself of habitual ways of expressing your anger that consistently cause trouble for you. These habits can be broken. A good psychotherapist can be of invaluable assistance in your struggle to transform your anger into a tool for making peace.

Conclusion

A World with Anger Under Control

I dream of a world with anger under control. It will be quite a different world from the one we live in now.

That certainly won't mean that you will suddenly never be angry again. You know how convinced I am that anger is an essential part of healthy living—and absolutely necessary for our survival. You and I, and everyone else in the world, will always need to be angry periodically.

But in the world I dream of, our anger will be used constructively to manage those problems which will be an inevitable consequence of our living together. There will be an end to the viciousness with which we often relate to each other—and a dramatic reduction of the major problems in our society which are related to our misguided anger expressions.

Is it absurd to dream of a world like that? Do you believe it to be a possibility? I do—not a strong possibility, mind you, but a possibility.

I'm convinced there is nothing we could do for the world that would be so helpful as to plan on a broad scale for the taming of our anger. If we could help ourselves and then help large numbers of other persons throughout the world to transform their anger into an ally for constructive living, we might start an unstoppable movement.

It's surely worth spending some time dreaming about.

What Will It Take?

If you wonder what it will take to create for yourself a world with anger under control, the answer undoubtedly centers on you. For you the world will never have its anger under control until you do. For one significant fact looms above all others: You are infinitely more vulnerable to your own anger than you are to anyone else's.

Once you have mastered your anger, then your world being under control will depend on the mastery efforts of those closest to you, the people to whom you expose yourself the most—your spouse, parents, intimate friends, children. "Your world" will benefit substantially with the developing expertise of each person on your "intimate list."

Beyond the tightly drawn little personal worlds, the big world having its anger under control will finally depend, I believe, on a massive national and international anger-management effort. What we need is for huge numbers of people all over the earth to recognize that their inability to handle anger is perhaps society's most threatening problem.

I think that could happen. The statistics about marriage breakdowns, child abuse, physical and emotional abuse of older persons, violent crime, psychosomatic ailments, and international crises are so dramatic that people are beginning to take notice. When experts speculate about the causes of these tragedies, the loudest voices I hear say: "It's our inability to handle anger. We have fallen victim to a dread disease—the assumption that our anger must be expressed aggressively. We simply do not know how to use anger constructively."

If these voices grow loud enough to reach into the power capitals of the world, there will come a call for help: "How can we extricate ourselves from this dilemma? How do we train our people to express their anger in the service of higher values? How do we intervene in anger-expression patterns which lead to such chaos?"

When this kind of national and international awareness occurs, the training of key groups in our society will become possible. Let me name the ten groups I would like to see trained in the management of their anger:

1. *Parents-to-be*—trained to express constructively their own anger and trained to teach their children to do the same.
2. *Kindergartners*—trained with effective modeling and reinforcement techniques to use their anger nonaggressively in the service of their values.
3. *Child, spouse, and older-person abusers*—referred by the courts, or self-referred, and required, or strongly encouraged, to complete an entire anger-management training program.
4. *Criminal offenders guilty of passionate violence*—again referred by the courts and required to complete the training program.
5. *Police cadets and on-duty policemen.* An effective training program for this group has already been developed by Dr. Raymond Novaco.[1]
6. *High school students*—as part of a regular required course.

[1] R. W. Novaco, "Training of probation counselors for anger problems." *Journal of Counseling Psychology*, 1980, 27, 385–90.

7. *Psychologists, psychiatrists, and all counselors and trainees within these categories*—as part of their professional training.

8. *Employment groups*—as part of the upgrading of their lives and their skills.

9. *Persons about to make major life changes*—as part of premarital, mid-life career change, or employment counseling programs.

10. *Media personnel*—from every branch of mass media—to prepare them effectively to communicate this training to large groups of persons.

Once these groups have been trained, we may expect a significant decrease in anger-motivated aggression.

Then we should concentrate on other influences which contribute to destructive anger expression. There are obviously many.

I would especially like for us to reassess the contributions which various types of activities make to the aggressiveness of our society. For instance, aggression-centered athletic contests such as football and ice hockey are examples of activities which should be analyzed for their modeling effects.

A world with anger under control—what will it take? It will certainly require that we make it a primary matter of national concern, and that as a part of that concern we train key groups to use their anger for the betterment of their own lives and the effective growth and development of the human family.

The Birth of Joy

In the Introduction I briefly discussed the intimate relationship of anger and joy. I have become convinced that when people learn to manage their anger in a constructive way, it is possible for them to enjoy life much more fully.

Almost everyone with whom I work is searching after joy. Without any question it is the finest of all human experiences. For when you are joyful, whatever your external state, you know deep within your core that rich sense of pleasure and delight.

I know some people who, even in the midst of physical suffering, have discovered joy. They are able to live in the center of an inner environment saturated by an intense, keenly felt, exuberant happiness.

How are they able to do that? How does anyone lay hold on joy in the middle of being human during times like these?

I am convinced that the answer can be found in the process of mastering anger. When you transform the enormous power which anger makes available and apply it to the problems in your life, you suddenly realize you don't have to remain trapped by painful experiences. You can break free of the hold of a miserable set of hurtful or frustrating events. You can clear your life of resentment-causing problems.

And this makes it possible for you to freely pursue the important goals in your life. The very freedom to do this will be enjoyable—and the reaching of these goals will be downright exhilarating.

But do you see my point? If you remain focused on the painful experiences in your life, how can there be any joy? And if you fail to use your anger effectively to dissolve and work through those experiences, how can you get free of them? I go so far as to say that until you have learned to handle your anger competently, there is no way you can experience joy.

But when you do learn to master that anger:

A. You are able to deal effectively with the hurt, frustration, and fear in your life. This "clears the tracks" for joy.
B. You experience yourself as having potency. You are able to manage your life adequately.
C. Thus, you never experience yourself as a victim of external events. There is no quality of "determined by others" about you.
D. You are in charge of your inner world! There is a sense of mastery about your experiencing.

This is a difficult world in which to live for all of us. We are regularly confronted with complicated and difficult to manage interpersonal events. But thank God, we also have available that magnificent inner capacity which prepares us to cope constructively. We call this capacity by the simple name of anger.

When we learn to use anger well, we are able to cope in a powerful way with these pain sources. And when we keep to a minimum the level of hurt and frustration in our lives, we are free to pursue intensively the state of joy.

Too many of us have spent too much of our lives trying to handle pain with our arms tied behind our backs. We have failed to express our anger constructively. Instead of dealing effectively with the source of our hurt, we have often created new reasons to be afraid or frustrated.

But no more! We are through with all of that. We know how to manage our anger now. No longer will it be able to master us. We are ready to take command.

I hope that you are beginning to experience the birth of joy in your life—a very fitting and deserved reward for all the effort you have expended in mastering your anger.

SELECTED READING

Alberti, R. E., and Emmons, M. L., *Your Perfect Right*. San Luis Obispo, Calif.: Impact, 1974.

Bach, G. R., and Goldberg, H., *Creative Aggression*. Garden City, N.Y.: Doubleday, 1974.

Bandura, A., *Aggression: A Social Learning Analysis*. Englewood Cliffs, N.J.: Prentice-Hall, 1973.

Baron, R. A., "Reducing the influence of an aggressive model: The restraining effects of discrepant modeling cues." *Journal of Personality and Social Psychology*, 1971, *20*, 240–45.

Becker, E., "Anthropological notes on the concept of aggression." *Psychiatry*, 1962, *25*, 328–38.

Berkowitz, L., ed., *Roots of Aggression*. New York: Atherton Press, 1969.

Berkowitz, L., "Experimental investigations of hostility catharsis." *Journal of Consulting and Clinical Psychology*, 1970, *35*, 1–7.

Delgado, J. M., "ESB." *Psychology Today*, 1970, *3*, 48–53.

Deutsch, M., "Conflicts: productive and destructive." *Journal of Social Issues*, 1969, *25*, 7–41.

Ellis, A., "Techniques of handling anger in marriage." *Journal of Marriage and Family Counseling*, 1976, *2*, 305–15.

Feshbach, S., "Dynamics and morality of violence and aggression." *American Psychologist*, 1971, *26*, 281–92.

Freud, S., *Civilization and Its Discontents*. (J. Strachey, ed. and trans.) New York: Norton, 1961.

Frodi, A., Macaulay, J., and Thome, P. R., "Are women always less aggressive than men? A review of the experimental literature." *Psychological Bulletin*, 1977, *84*, 634–60.

Gardner, R. A., "The Mutual Storytelling Technique in the treatment of anger-inhibition problems." *International Journal of Child Psychotherapy*, 1972, *1*, 34–64.

Hokanson, J. E., Willers, K. R., and Koropsak, E., "The modification of autonomic responses during aggressive interchange." *Journal of Personality*, 1968, *36*, 386.

Konecni, V. J., "Annoyance, type, and duration of postannoyance activity, and aggression: The 'cathartic effect.'" *Journal of Experimental Psychology: General*, 1975, *104*, 76–102.

Luborsky, L., Docherty, J. P., and Penick, S., "Onset conditions for psychosomatic symposium: A comparative review of immediate observation with retrospective research." *Psychosomatic Medicine*, 1973, *35*, 187–204.

Novaco, R. W., *Anger Control*. Lexington, Mass.: Lexington Books, 1975.

——, "Training of probation counselors for anger problems." *Journal of Counseling Psychology*, 1980, *27*, 385–90.

Mace, D. R., "Marital intimacy and the deadly love-anger cycle." *Journal of Marriage and Family Counseling*, 1976, *2*, 131–37.

Madow, L., *Anger*. New York: Scribner's, 1972.

Rubin, T. I., *The Angry Book*. New York: Macmillan, 1969.

Rule, B. G., and Nesdale, A. R., "Emotional arousal and aggressive behavior." *Psychological Bulletin*, 1976, *83*, 851–63.

Sandler, J., and Quagliano, J., "Punishment in a signal avoidance situation." Paper presented at the meeting of the Southeastern Psychological Association, Gatlinburg, Tenn., 1964.

Saul, L. J., "A psychoanalytic view of hostility: Its genesis, treatment, and implications for society." *Humanitas*, 1976, *12*, 171–82.

Scheier, M. F., "Self-awareness, self-consciousness, and angry aggression." *Journal of Personality*, 1976, *44*, 627–44.

Seligman, M. E. P., Maier, S. F., and Geer, J. H., "Alleviation of learned helplessness in the dog." *Journal of Abnormal Psychology*, 1968, *73*, No. 3, 256–62.

Schimmel, S., "Anger and its control in Graeco-Roman and modern psychology." *Psychiatry*, 1979, *42*, 320–37.

Straus, M. A., Gelles, R. J., and Steinmetz, S. K., *Behind Closed Doors*. Garden City, N.Y.: Anchor Press/Doubleday, 1981.

NEIL CLARK WARREN has a Ph.D. in Psychology from the University of Chicago and is founding partner of Associated Psychological Services in Pasadena, California. Until recently the Dean of the Graduate School of Psychology at Fuller Theological Seminary, Dr. Warren is now engaged full-time in private practice and in conducting seminaries on the mastery of anger all over the country.

For more information regarding Dr. Warren and his Anger Management Seminars, and especially speaking availability, you may contact him at 595 East Colorado Boulevard, Pasadena, California, 91101.